THE TITANIC

A READER'S DIGEST BOOK

Edited and Produced by Carlton Books Limited

Project Editor: Simon Kirrane
Senior Art Editor: Diane Klein
Picture Researcher: Lorna Ainger
Production: Sarah Schuman

The credits that appear on page 128 are hereby made a part of this copyright page

Library of Congress Cataloging in Publication Data
Tibballs, Geoff.
    The Titanic : the extraordinary story of the "unsinkable" ship/Geoff Tibballs.
        p.   cm.
    Includes index.
    ISBN 0-89577-990-0 (hardcover). — ISBN 0-89577-953-6 (pbk.)
    1. Titanic (Steamship) 2. Shipwrecks—North Atlantic Ocean.
    I. Title.
G530.T6T54 1997
363.12'3'091631—dc21   97-14175

Reader's Digest and the Pegasus logo are trademarks of The Reader's Digest Association, Inc.
Sixth Printing, July 1998

THE TITANIC

THE EXTRAORDINARY STORY OF THE UNSINKABLE SHIP

Geoff Tibballs

Reader's Digest

THE READER'S DIGEST ASSOCIATION, INC.

Pleasantville, New York/Montreal

CONTENTS

INTRODUCTION
THE LURE
AND THE LORE

She is the most famous ship in the world. The *Golden Hind*, the *Mayflower*, H.M.S. *Victory*, the *QE2* have earned their places in history, but somehow they all pale in comparison with the *Titanic*. Yet she made only one voyage, in April 1912, which ended in disaster. In the icy waters of the North Atlantic in the dead of night, the *Titanic* struck an iceberg and went down with the loss of some 1,523 lives.

A BRUSH WITH DESTINY *Leaving Southampton, the* **Titanic** *almost collides with another liner, the* **New York.**

Eighty-five years later, her legend is as strong as ever. The word "titanic" has become part of our vocabulary, often synonymous with an epic struggle doomed to failure. Books are still written (more than 3,000 to date), films continue to be made and societies still exist to debate how the supposedly invincible liner was laid to rest at the bottom of the ocean.

The *Titanic* was no ordinary ship — she was a floating hotel, even a small town at sea. At the time of her launch in Belfast in 1911, she was not only the biggest existing ship, but was also the largest movable object ever built. A glorious Edwardian extravagance designed to sweep aside competition to the White Star Line on the lucrative Atlantic routes, she was the ultimate symbol of luxury and power. This opulence was reflected in the passenger list for her maiden voyage from Southampton to New York. The cream of American society was on board, eager to be part of a journey that would surely be talked about for years to come. Tragically, they were to be proved right.

Enduring fascination

As with so many legends, the stories surrounding the sinking of the *Titanic* have been embellished over the years, making it difficult to determine fact from fiction. Dark rumors abound: that first-class passengers commandeered the few available lifeboats at the expense of the lower classes; that one cowardly man escaped the sinking ship by dressing as a woman; that the *Titanic* perished partly because she was attempting a record time for crossing the Atlantic; and that all, or most of, the dead, could have been saved had the nearby cargo vessel, the *Californian,* reacted to the *Titanic's* distress rockets. While a breakdown of the death toll reveals that chances of survival were much greater among first-class passengers than among third-class (or steerage), there is no evidence of any malpractice by the upper classes. On the contrary, the majority behaved impeccably. As for the man in the cunning disguise, it appears it was nothing more than a male passenger putting a shawl over his head to keep out the cold and being briefly mistaken for a woman. Nor was the *Titanic* aiming for a record crossing, although she may have been traveling too fast for the conditions. And the case against the *Californian* remains, as we shall see later, inconclusive.

There are still sufficient verified images to ensure that the *Titanic* legend is perpetuated for many years to come: the ship's orchestra playing on, as all around them fled for their lives; four first-class passengers in evening dress continuing to play bridge after the fateful collision; the captain gallantly going down with his ship; and the unidentified "mystery ship" whose lights were seen by survivors in the vicinity of the disaster before it veered off into the distance.

Perhaps most poignant of all are the grainy black-and-white photographs showing the massive liner

fully lit against the evening sky as she arrived at Cherbourg, her first port of call after Southampton. Her sheer magnitude is a sight to behold and is all the more compelling when viewed with hindsight, knowing the fate that was to await her four days later. For many, however, the enduring fascination with the *Titanic* lies in the numerous coincidences and psychic phenomena connected with the disaster — a list that would not be out of place in *The X Files*.

The most remarkable chain of coincidence can be found in *Futility (or The Wreck of the Titan),* an obscure novel written by retired Merchant Navy officer Morgan Robertson in 1898, 14 years before

ALMOST SPECTRAL
At the first port of call on her maiden voyage, the **Titanic's** *glowing silhouette dominates the sky.*

FOREWORD

The novel **Futility** *tells an uncannily prophetic tale of a liner and an iceberg.*

the *Titanic*'s maiden voyage. The action revolved around the *Titan*, a huge, supposedly unsinkable British liner. On its maiden voyage from Southampton to New York in April, with 2,000 people on board, it was attempting a record crossing when its starboard hull was severely pierced by an iceberg in the North Atlantic, causing it to sink. There were only 13 survivors, the vast loss of life caused primarily by shortage of lifeboats, precisely the charge that would be leveled at the owners of the *Titanic*. Robertson's choice of name for his ship is coincidental enough, but when one takes into account that both ships sailed in the same month, both had triple-screw propellers and a top speed of 24–25 knots, both were of near identical size and displacement, both were carrying approximately the same number of people, and both were on maiden voyages when they encountered an identical problem in the same stretch of water, it then becomes an eerily accurate prediction of the *Titanic* disaster that defies any logical explanation.

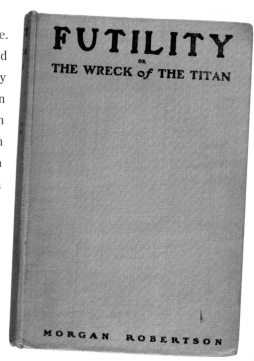

Another prophetic novel was *From the Old World to the New* written in 1892 by noted British journalist and spiritualist W. T. Stead. His nautical tale also told of the sinking of a ship after striking an iceberg in the North Atlantic. A number of survivors were picked up by a passing vessel, *Majestic*, captained by E. J. Smith. Twenty years later, the ill-fated captain of the *Titanic* was also named

W. T. STEAD

Did the spiritualist foresee his own death?

E. J. Smith. As for Stead, he too went down with the *Titanic*.

The real Captain Smith had suffered a string of misfortunes prior to skippering the *Titanic*, a sequence of events that he superstitiously attributed to a malevolent sea kelpie (in Scottish folklore, a water spirit in the form of a horse). In September 1911, he had been in charge of the *Olympic*, the sister ship to the *Titanic*, when she collided with the British cruiser H.M.S. *Hawke* off the Isle of Wight and suffered extensive damage. Still under Captain Smith's command, *Olympic* collided with a sunken wreck while making the crossing from New York to Southampton on February 2, 1912. After being put into dry-dock at Belfast for repairs, she was about to return to the Atlantic when she became grounded on rocks and was forced to return to dry-dock for further repairs. Captain Smith was subsequently transferred to the *Titanic*, but as the great ship left Southampton on April 10, 1912, she was involved in a dramatic near-miss with the moored liner *New York*. Many viewed it as a dreadful omen for a new ship. Four days later, their fears were horribly justified. Ironically, Smith had become so disenchanted with his misfortune that he had decided he would retire after the *Titanic*'s maiden voyage.

Superstition and premonition

Some passengers boarding the ship at its second port of call, Queenstown in Ireland, saw further cause for alarm. Superstitious Catholics were horrified to spot the hull number 3909 04 beneath her name on the *Titanic*'s bow, since a mirror-image of these numbers would, with a little imagination, read "NO POPE." To heighten their anxiety, they knew that the liner had been built in Belfast, a city that was then, as now, divided by religious bigotry.

Another strange coincidence occurs in the May

1912 issue of *Popular* magazine, which contained a short story about a great liner ramming an iceberg in the North Atlantic. The magazine was rolling off the presses just as *Titanic* was preparing to leave Southampton. It is said that the author, who wrote under the name of Mayn Clew Garnett, had dreamed the details of his story while on a recent voyage on board the *Olympic*.

"They say it's unsinkable ..."

The eight-man orchestra on the *Titanic*, all of whom played on heroically until the sea swept them away to their deaths, have passed into folklore as the epitome of the stiff upper lip in crises. John Hume, a 21-year-old Scottish violinist, had been on board *Olympic* when she collided with H.M.S. *Hawke*, an incident that prompted a great foreboding in his mother. She

begged him so hard not to go back to sea that he told several friends about it. After the disaster, one friend revealed that Mrs. Hume had dreamed that something terrible would happen to her son on the *Titanic* trip.

Mrs. Hume was not the only person to experience a dreadful premonition about the *Titanic*. Many others expressed the view that something dreadful would happen. Some of these claims can be dismissed as standard misgivings about the sea or maiden voyages, but others refer more explicitly to *Titanic*.

When American theater producer Henry B. Harris cabled home that he and his wife had booked to travel on the *Titanic*, his business associate William Klein was filled with such a sense of impending doom that he promptly sent a cable to Harris, imploring him not to sail on the great liner. Harris replied that it was too late to change his plans and he and his wife duly boarded the ship. As the *Titanic* sank into the icy seas, Harris kissed his wife

goodbye and helped her into the last lifeboat. He then went down with the ship.

The Rouse family, from Sittingbourne in Kent, were due to emigrate to the United States in 1912. Originally, the whole family were to travel together, but Richard Rouse decided to sail ahead so that he could arrange everything by the time his wife Charity and eight-year-old daughter Gladys arrived. He reserved a berth on the *Titanic* and a week or so before departure, took his wife and daughter to Southampton to view the great vessel. Mrs. Rouse was overcome with fear and told her husband, "That ship is too big. I have a bad feeling that it will never reach America." She tried to talk him out of going, but he replied, "Don't worry. It's a brand new ship and, besides, they say it's unsinkable." But Mrs. Rouse continued to worry, even after receiving a reassuring postcard from her husband, posted at either Cherbourg or Queenstown. A couple of days later, she fainted when she heard the *Titanic* had gone down in the Atlantic. Her husband was not among the survivors.

In the spring of 1912, Stephen Jenkin was set to return to the United States from his parents' home in Cornwall. He had already booked his passage on a ship, but a coal strike forced a change of plan and his reservation was switched to the *Titanic*. On learning this, he became increasingly worried about his own safety and, after setting off for Southampton, he suddenly decided to return to his parents' home. There, he removed all of his valuables, including his watch, and left them with his parents, in case he was killed on the crossing. Sure enough, Stephen Jenkin was among those who died on the *Titanic*.

"It is doomed. I feel it! I know it!"

Mrs. William Bucknell of Philadelphia was due to board *Titanic* at Cherbourg with Mrs. J. J. Brown, who earned the title "The Unsinkable Molly Brown" for her bravery. But Mrs. Bucknell had an awful premonition and told her friend, "I'm deathly afraid to go aboard that ship. I feel sure something terrible is going to happen." Even when persuaded by Mrs. Brown to board the ship as planned, Mrs. Bucknell

SIREN SONG
Having been on board **Olympic** *when she collided with* **H.M.S.** **Hawke,** *what drew violinist John Hume to join the maiden voyage of her sister ship, the* **Titanic***?*

persisted. "It is doomed," she said. "I feel it! I know it!" On the evening of April 14, she repeated her fears to Philadelphia physician Dr. Arthur Brewe in the ship's first-class dining room. The two women then retired to their staterooms. Their next encounter was on deck after the collision with the iceberg, by which time both were wearing lifebelts. Mrs. Bucknell exclaimed, "Didn't I tell you? I knew it." The two women lived to tell their tale, but Dr. Brewe perished.

New York lawyer Isaac C. Frauenthal had traveled to Europe for the wedding of his brother Henry in Nice. The brothers and Henry's bride sailed home on the *Titanic*. Shortly after leaving Southampton, Isaac Frauenthal revealed a dream he had had before boarding the ship: "It seemed to me that I was on a big steamship that suddenly crashed into something and began to go down. I saw in the dream as vividly as I could see with open eyes the gradual settling of the ship, and I heard the cries and shouts of frightened passengers." He might have dismissed this as nothing more than an ordinary nightmare but for the fact that he subsequently had exactly the

FINAL PORT OF CALL
The **Titanic** *leaves Queenstown harbor, Ireland, after taking on the mail.*

same dream. So when, on the fateful night of April 14, he got out of bed and discovered that the *Titanic* had hit an iceberg, he was all too aware of the danger. His brother Henry was unmoved, insisting that the ship was too big to sink, but Isaac persisted and the three managed to escape in a lifeboat.

"That ship is going to sink"

One of the most emphatic premonitions was that of Mrs. Blanche Marshall, who watched with her family, friends and servants as the *Titanic* steamed past the Isle of Wight shortly after leaving Southampton. Suddenly she declared, "That ship is going to sink before it reaches America." Everyone reminded her that the *Titanic* was unsinkable, but she snapped, "I can see hundreds of people struggling in the icy water. Are you all so blind that you are going to let them drown?" Three years later, Mrs. Marshall also correctly predicted that the *Lusitania* would sink on its May voyage, after being hit by a German torpedo.

In a few instances, the sense of foreboding was so great that prospective passengers were actually persuaded to change their minds about sailing on the *Titanic*. Seattle violinist Frank Adelman had booked for himself and his wife to return to America aboard the great ship, but a few days before departure, Mrs. Adelman had a sudden premonition of danger and urged her husband to cancel the booking and travel on a later passage. Mr. Adelman agreed to toss a coin to decide whether they should travel as planned or

FADING VISION
For three-quarters of those aboard, this stretch of Irish coast was to be their last glimpse of land.

stationed at Kirkcudbright in Scotland. At 11:00PM local time on the night of April 14, 1912, he sat at the bedside of a dying orphan girl named Jessie and listened as she predicted the great tragedy that would unfold in the Atlantic three and a half hours later. Grasping his hand, she exclaimed, "Can't you see that big ship sinking in the water?" Captain Sowden explained that it was probably just a bad dream, but the girl was adamant. "Look at all those people who are drowning," she continued. "Someone called Wally is playing a fiddle and coming to you." With that, the girl fell into a coma, but shortly before she died, Captain Sowden heard the sound of the latch on the bedroom door followed by the sensation that an invisible being had entered the room. Captain Sowden said, "Some hours later, the whole world was startled by the tragedy of the *Titanic*. Among those drowned was Wally Hartley, its bandmaster, whom I knew well as a boy. I had no knowledge of his going to sea or having anything to do with any ship."

Truth stranger than fiction

And so the legend of the *Titanic* lives on, fueled by the mystery that surrounds it. In 1985, the wreck of the liner was discovered beneath the Atlantic by an expedition led by American oceanographer Dr. Robert Ballard. The exploration of the wreck should have yielded many answers, but the presence of a mysterious bulkhead and the absence of the stern nameplate has merely produced another theory on how the *Titanic* went to her grave. In 1995, authors Robin Gardiner and Dan van der Vat published their conclusions in *The Riddle of the Titanic*, a book described by some critics as from the same school that suggests that Elvis Presley is alive and well and working at McDonald's.

Gardiner and van der Vat claim the *Titanic* never sank, but that it was her sister ship, the *Olympic*, which went down as part of a £1 million insurance fraud hatched by John Pierpont Morgan, owner of the White Star Line. Intriguingly, Morgan canceled his reservation on the ship at the last minute. The authors allege that the conspiracy began in 1911, when the *Olympic* was damaged in the collision with the cruiser

"LOOK AT ALL THOSE PEOPLE WHO ARE DROWNING"
A dying girl predicts a terrible tragedy at sea.

wait. Fortunately for them both, Mrs. Adelman won the toss and they canceled their booking on the *Titanic*. An equally persuasive wife was a Mrs. Shepherd of Nebraska who, after experiencing a dream in which the *Titanic* sank, begged her husband by letter and cable to take another ship. He accordingly canceled his reservation on the doomed liner in favor of another White Star steamship.

Salvation Army captain W. Rex Sowden was

H.M.S. *Hawke*. White Star was unable to recover the repair costs and was left with a weakened vessel. It was allegedly patched up and switched with the nearly completed *Titanic* before being deliberately sailed at high speed into the icefields of the North Atlantic. The plan, say the authors, was to glance an iceberg and open the sluices, allowing time for an orderly evacuation to a strategically placed White Star vessel — the "mystery ship" whose lights were reported nearby, but never identified. However, it is said the *Olympic* hit an iceberg too hard, too soon. It is an interesting, if unlikely, theory and one that helps maintain an interest in the sinking of the *Titanic*.

Genuinely corroborated events have also played their part. In April 1935, a ship called *Titanian*, carrying coal from Newcastle to Canada, almost suffered the same fate as the *Titanic* when it encountered an iceberg in the same area of the North Atlantic. Luckily, crewman William Reeves had a premonition of impending disaster and yelled "Danger ahead!" to the navigator shortly before the iceberg became visible in the darkness. Strangely, Reeves was born on April 15, 1912, the day the *Titanic* sank.

One thing is certain — where the *Titanic* is concerned, truth really is stranger than fiction.

THE LAST STOP
The **Titanic** *is pictured here off the coast of Queenstown (now Cobh) her last port of call.*

CHAPTER ONE

THE BIGGEST
SHIP IN THE
WORLD

At the turn of the century, Lord Pirrie and Joseph Bruce Ismay were two of the most powerful men in the shipping world. Pirrie was chairman of Harland & Wolff, the renowned Belfast shipbuilding firm, and Ismay was chairman of one of Britain's greatest steamship companies, the White Star Line.

GREAT HOPES *Harland & Wolff strengthened its slipways to build a new generation of liner.*

The White Star Line was locked in a fierce battle with the Cunard Line for control of the hugely profitable North Atlantic run between Britain and the United States. Harland & Wolff had always built the White Star ships, so the two men knew each other well. And both recognized that expansion was the only way to defeat Cunard.

One evening in 1907, Ismay dined with Lord and Lady Pirrie at their London residence, Devonshire House in Mayfair. After dinner, Pirrie casually proposed the construction of three vast transatlantic liners — far bigger, faster, and more luxurious than anything currently afloat. As Ismay listened enthusiastically, Pirrie drew up rough plans for the three liners. To reflect their size and class, they were to be called *Olympic*, *Titanic,* and *Gigantic*. The latter, renamed the *Britannic*, was sunk by a German mine in 1916, by which time the first two ships in this mighty triumvirate had become household names — but for very different reasons.

Belfast had a fine tradition of shipbuilding dating back to the mid-nineteenth century. The yards were built on artificial land at Queen's Island, reclaimed by the Belfast port authority between 1841 and 1846 during the construction of the Victoria Channel. Some of this land was leased to the firm Robert Hickson & Co., which began building iron sailing ships there in 1853. The following year, Yorkshire engineer Edward Harland joined as manager and when Hickson retired in 1858, Harland bought the business for the sum of £5,000.

Harland introduced new ideas to the craft of shipbuilding. He did away with wooden upper decks, preferring iron decks, which turned the hull into an extremely strong box girder. He also changed the shape of the hulls by incorporating a flat bottom and square bilges to increase the ships' capacities. Harland was fortunate to receive financial backing from Gustavus Schwabe, a German Jew who had invested in a small Liverpool shipping firm, the Bibby Line. Schwabe gave repair and building contracts to Harland. The new yard's first contract was for three steamers for the Bibby Line — a sizable order. On January 1, 1862, Schwabe's nephew, an engineer called Gustav Wolff, became Harland's partner and the famous firm Harland & Wolff was in business.

Rise of William James Pirrie

Among its first crop of apprentices was a 15-year-old Canadian boy, William James Pirrie. Born in Quebec, he was the son of an Ulsterman of Scottish descent. His mother also hailed from Ulster. When his father died, young Pirrie returned to Ireland with his mother and joined Harland & Wolff. Pirrie progressed through the ranks swiftly — from draftsman, assistant manager, sub-manager, works manager and, by the time he was 27, to partner. By then, Harland & Wolff was a major player; the energy and enterprise of the partners and a high standard of work had established an enviable reputation. In 1864, the gross tonnage of ships built at the yard was 30,000. By 1884, the figure had risen to 104,000.

Pirrie's career coincided with the development of steel shipbuilding. When Harland died in 1895, Pirrie took over as chairman. Eleven years later, Wolff retired, leaving Pirrie (who by then had been raised to the peerage) in total command. Pirrie was a dictator in all but name. An energetic little man, he secured the orders for ships himself and then had them built largely to his own designs, his clients offering little more than general specifications. Nobody other than Pirrie knew about or was permitted to discuss the firm's finances. Under Pirrie's driving force, the yard underwent considerable modernization between 1906 and 1908. Two enlarged building slips were constructed in an area where there had previously been three. A huge gantry, covering an area 840 feet by 240 feet, was erected over the two new slipways. These would house *Olympic* and *Titanic*, the first two of the three great liners to be built following Pirrie's deal with the White Star Line and J. Bruce Ismay.

WILLIAM JAMES PIRRIE
By the age of 27, he had become a partner in Harland & Wolff.

SISTERS
The **Olympic** *and the* **Titanic** *emerged from the Harland & Wolff yard within months of each other.*

Profits in the Atlantic

The White Star flag was first flown around 1850 by a line of sailing vessels that carried hopeful British emigrants to Australia, where gold had just been discovered. In 1867, the owner of the line retired and the fleet subsequently passed into the hands of Thomas Henry Ismay, son of a Cumberland boatbuilder. Ismay set about replacing wooden sailing ships with iron vessels and enlisted the financial support of Gustavus Schwabe. While the Australian run was profitable, both Ismay and Schwabe realized that even greater rewards lay in the route across the Atlantic.

This pot of gold was created by the rapid expansion of the United States in the second half of the nineteenth century. Between 1840, when Samuel Cunard's *Britannia* began the first transatlantic steamship service, and 1890, trade between the United States and Britain increased sevenfold, principally in cotton, tobacco, and wheat. At the

same time, the population of the United States quadrupled. Cunard had been concentrating solely on ferrying mail, cargo, and first-class passengers, but now there was a whole new clientele of lower-class, steerage passengers — British and European emigrants eager to sample life on the other side of the Atlantic. Not everyone liked what they saw and in some years as many as 100,000 disillusioned Britons headed back home. And the only way they could travel was by ship. To accommodate this surge of interest, passenger lists grew longer and ships grew bigger.

Given Schwabe's involvement in both camps, it was inevitable that White Star's ships would be built at Harland & Wolff. The association began with *Oceanic* in 1870. She was 420 feet long, 41 feet wide and 31 feet deep, with a tonnage of 3,707, and she embodied a number of design improvements previously unknown in the Atlantic trade. Further vessels followed, so that White Star was soon challenging Cunard on the Atlantic routes. By 1875, White Star ships such as *Britannic* and *Germanic* could attain speeds of more than 16 knots, thus reducing the journey time to under seven and a half days. In 1889, White Star introduced its first twin-screw steamers, *Teutonic* and *Majestic*, both of which could travel at 20 knots. As other shipowners observed the healthy competition, they joined the fray — notably the Germans.

America was also keen to get in on the act. Shipping had been slow to develop in the United States, partly because of the American Civil War and partly because potential financiers were investing instead in oil, steel and the railroads. Then, despite the efforts of T. H. Ismay, Inman Lines of Liverpool was sold to the International Navigation Company of Philadelphia and the Pennsylvania Railroad Company, enabling the Americans to gain access to superior British technology. The new company later came under the wing of American financier John Pierpont Morgan.

Bitter price war

Morgan immediately set about conquering the Atlantic by ruthlessly vanquishing all forms of competition. After achieving an amalgamation with the leading German lines, he turned his attention to Cunard by starting a price war. Morgan offered third-class transatlantic passages for as little as £2. Cunard's horror was heightened when Morgan then attempted to buy the company, only to find himself thwarted by the British government who reacted quickly to prevent another British company falling into American hands.

At Harland & Wolff, Pirrie realized that Morgan posed a serious threat to the yard's livelihood. A continuation of the price war would mean there

JOHN PIERPONT MORGAN
The aggressive American entrepreneur acquired the White Star line and was therefore the real owner of the **Titanic.**

would be less money to spend on building new ships. Besides, much of Pirrie's business came from White Star, which was just as vulnerable as Cunard. He had also lost a number of his allies. Schwabe had died in 1890 and T. H. Ismay in 1899. Now Ismay's son, J. Bruce Ismay, was at the helm of White Star, but he was inexperienced compared with such a brash entrepreneur as Morgan. So Pirrie decided to join forces with Morgan and in 1902 he helped him acquire White Star. From then on, White Star was a subsidiary of International Mercantile Marine, of which Morgan was proprietor. J. Bruce Ismay remained with White Star as chairman and all White Star ships continued to have British crews and to fly the British flag, but the real power lay on the other side of the Atlantic.

Bigger and faster

The trend towards bigger and faster ships had been a feature of nineteenth-century maritime history. The first vessel to cross the Atlantic continuously under steam power was the *Sirius* in 1838. A small wooden paddle steamer — 208 feet long, 25 feet wide and with a depth of hold of 18 feet — she averaged a speed of just seven and a half knots. She was less

JOSEPH BRUCE ISMAY
The chairman of White Star, he was later pilloried for his behavior as the **Titanic** *went down.*

than a quarter of the size of the *Titanic*. As technology improved, wooden hulls were replaced first by iron and then by steel. In the wake of Brunel's 1858 white elephant the *Great Eastern*, paddle wheels were discarded as a means of propulsion in favor of the screw propeller driven by reciprocating engines. In turn, the reciprocating engine developed from the compound- to the triple- and later to the quadruple-expansion type in order to provide greater power and a faster crossing.

SETTING THE STANDARD
The Cunarder **Mauretania** *represented a new breed of liner. To survive, White Star had to come up with a better one.*

All the while, the ships were getting bigger and bigger. Cunard built the *Bothnia* of 4,555 tons in 1874, followed by the 7,718-ton *Umbria* in 1884 and, nine years later, the 12,950-ton *Campania*. White Star responded with the 9,686-ton *Teutonic* and *Majestic* in 1890 and then, in 1899, another *Oceanic*, which this time was 685 feet long, with a tonnage of 17,274.

The battle between the big two intensified in the early years of the twentieth century. Before his death in 1899, Thomas Ismay had planned four large liners for White Star, each emphasizing comfort rather than speed. J. Bruce Ismay carried out his father's wishes with *Celtic* (1901), *Cedric* (1903), *Baltic* (1904), and the mighty 709 foot-long, 25,541-ton *Adriatic* in 1907. Cunard's answer was bigger and better. Heavily subsidized by the British government, who were alarmed by the spate of mighty German liners, Cunard produced two splendid new ships which, the government hoped, could prove invaluable in the event of war. Launched in 1907, the *Lusitania* and the *Mauretania* were larger and faster than any other vessel. Furthermore, they featured an innovative method of propulsion — the steam turbine. More economical and more powerful than the traditional piston-based reciprocating engine, the steam turbine proved an immediate success. White Star knew it had to match its rival — and fast — otherwise trade would suffer.

A grand design

At the time, White Star ran a regular service from Southampton to New York with *Teutonic*, *Oceanic*, and *Adriatic*, but these could not compete for speed with the Cunarders, which were capable of an average speed of 26 knots. At 21 knots, the *Teutonic* was the fastest of the White Star ships. To attempt to increase a ship's speed would necessitate restricting passenger and cargo space, clearly an uneconomical move. So White Star elected for a different option — it would construct a fleet of huge liners whose spacious accommodation and overwhelming luxury would prove irresistible to passengers. Not only would first-class passengers be treated in accordance with the finest hotels, but even steerage travelers would find far better facilities than on other transatlantic liners. And so, backed by American finance, Lord Pirrie and J. Bruce Ismay sat down over coffee and cigars that evening in 1907 to plan the construction of three great liners. At 850 feet, each would be 100 feet longer than the Cunarders and, at 46,000 tons, they would be 15,000 tons heavier. They would revolutionize transatlantic travel. The emphasis would be on elegance and, above all, safety, an achievement of which White Star was justifiably proud. Between 1902 and 1912, the line carried 2,179,594 passengers, of whom only two were killed.

Pirrie's grandiose plans appeared to have just one flaw. No dock or yard was large enough for the ships' construction. But Pirrie was not to be deterred and so the two specially strengthened slipways were built at Harland & Wolff. Meanwhile, detailed plans for the liners were drawn up by a team of designers, led by Lord Pirrie's brother-in-law, Alexander Carlisle, who expanded the hull design he had produced for the second *Oceanic*. It was Carlisle, Harland & Wolff's general manager, who would also be responsible for the ships' interiors and their life-saving equipment. When he retired in 1910, he was succeeded by another of Pirrie's relatives, his nephew Thomas Andrews.

The design was presented to White Star management when J. Bruce Ismay visited Belfast on July 29, 1908. He gave the design his approval and a contract was signed for the building of the first two ships. Work on keel number 400, that of the *Olympic*, began on December 16, 1908 at Harland & Wolff's number two slipway Keel number 401, the future *Titanic*, was laid at slipway three on March 31, 1909.

As sister ships, the *Olympic* and *Titanic* were virtually identical in their basic construction. They had four huge funnels and were triple-screw steamers, powered by two sets of four-cylinder reciprocating engines, each driving a wing propeller and with a 420-ton low-pressure turbine driving the center propeller by

ALEXANDER CARLISLE
He led the team that designed White Star's three great liners.

TITANIC SPECIFICATIONS

Overall length: 882 feet 9 inches	
Beam: 92 feet 6 inches	
Molded depth: 59 feet 6 inches	
Total height from keel to navigating bridge: 104 feet	
Tonnage: 46,328 (gross)	
Displacement: 66,000 tons	
Decks: 10	
Boilers: 29	
Furnaces: 159	
Engines: 2 triple expansion, 1 turbine	
Total horsepower: 46,000	
Service speed: 21 knots	
Maximum speed: 24-25 knots	
Maximum number of passengers and crew: 3,547	
Number of lifeboats: 20 (1,176 places)	

recycling steam from the main engines. The two outer propellers each had three blades, the center propeller had four. The main engines produced 15,000 horsepower apiece, with the turbine engine adding another 16,000hp. This extra power was enough to give a top speed of 24 to 25 knots. The steam came from 29 boilers (24 double-ended and five single-ended) situated in six boiler-rooms and each watertight boiler compartment had its own pumping equipment. The double-ended boilers measured 20 feet long, 15 feet 9 inches in diameter and contained six furnaces; the single-ended boilers were the same diameter, but only 11 feet 9 inches long and containing just three furnaces. There were

IN THE SHADOW OF GIANTS
Under construction, White Star's liners towered 100 feet over Belfast.

159 furnaces in total, fueled from a series of coal-bunkers with a combined capacity of more than 8,000 tons. Almost the entire space beneath upper deck E was occupied by the steam-generating plant, the coal-bunkers and the propelling machinery. The bunkers were arranged so that handling the fuel for each boiler was reduced to a minimum. Of the four funnels, the foremost three catered for the boiler-rooms, while the fourth was used for ventilation.

Communication below decks was achieved via a system of illuminated telegraphs linking the starting platform and the various boiler-rooms. This enabled the engineer on watch to issue his orders with speed and efficiency.

Rigid and watertight

The ships' skeletons consisted of a series of vertical frames, each set a yard apart from stem to stern and criss-crossed by beams, girders, and pillars. At the bow, the frames were just 2 feet apart and at the stern the interval was 2 feet 3 inches. A feature of both ships was their double bottom, hailed as an important safety device. The outer skin, made of inch-thick steel plates, shielded an inner skin of slightly thinner plates, the belief being that if the outer skin was somehow pierced, water would still be kept at bay by the inner skin. The double bottom was deep enough for a man to walk along upright. Half a million solid iron rivets, fitted hydraulically and weighing 270 tons, were used just on the bottom of the *Titanic*, with a total of three million fitted on the whole ship. No expense was spared as far as riveting was concerned. The seams of the bottom plating were double-riveted and those on the topside plating were treble- and quadruple-riveted. The butts of the bottom plating were overlapped and quadruple riveted.

To reduce rolling in heavy seas, a pair of 25-inch-deep bilge-keels were fitted for 300 feet of the vessel's length amidships on either side of the bottom. Special steel castings, supplied by the Darlington Forge Company, were made to brace the stern and to support the three propellers and the cast-steel rudder. The six pieces of the rudder, which measured 78 feet 8 inches long and 15 feet 3 inches wide, together weighed more than 101 tons.

The beams of the bridge, shelter, saloon, and upper decks amidships were supported by four longitudinal girders, which in turn were supported by solid round pillars spaced 9 feet apart. The two decks forming the superstructure of the ship and the navigating bridge were built to ensure a high degree of rigidity. At the sides, they were supported on built-up frames in line with the hull frames, but at wider intervals. The deckhouses were specially stiffened by channel-section steel fitted in the frame work. In certain areas, particularly where there were passengers' rooms, heavy brackets were introduced to ensure a smoother passage through choppy waters.

To all intents and purposes, the *Titanic* was watertight. In addition to the double bottom, she was divided into 16 watertight compartments, formed by 15 watertight bulkheads running across the hull. Six of these reached up to D deck, eight went up to E deck and the other one rose only as far as F deck. Each bulkhead was equipped with automatic watertight doors. These were held in the open position by a friction clutch that could be released instantly by a powerful electric magnet controlled from the captain's bridge. In the event of an accident, the captain could move the electric switch and close all doors to make the ship 100 per cent watertight. As a further precaution, floats were provided beneath floor level. Should water enter any of the compartments, these floats would automatically lift and close the doors opening into that compartment if they had not already been dropped by the captain. It was also claimed the ship could float with any two compartments flooded and since nobody could envisage anything worse, the *Titanic* was deemed unsinkable.

Aura of invincibility

This belief was strengthened in articles written to celebrate the ship's launch in 1911. The esteemed organ *The Shipbuilder* published a special issue in which it described the watertight compartments and electrically controlled doors. The article concluded: "In the event of an accident, or at any time when it may be considered advisable, the captain can, by simply moving an electric switch, instantly close the doors throughout, practically making the vessel unsinkable."

The aura of invincibility had been created. What observers failed to note in their haste to praise the splendid-looking ship was that *Titanic*'s bulkheads were carried just 10 feet above the waterline, compared with 30 feet on Brunel's *Great Eastern*. When, in 1862, the latter had a huge gash, 83 feet long and 9 feet wide, ripped in her outer skin after scraping a rock, she did not sink. The *Titanic* was to suffer comparable damage, yet it spelled her demise. Even the system of electrically controlled watertight doors

HARNESSING THE ENERGY
15,000 horsepower was transmitted by each of the **Titanic's** *main propeller shafts.*

was not as impressive as it sounded. In truth, only 12 doors at the very bottom of the *Titanic* could be closed automatically — the majority had to be closed by hand. Although they may have thought it to be the case, it is interesting to note that the ship's builders and owners refrained from describing the ship as "unsinkable" prior to her fateful maiden voyage.

But *The Shipbuilder* remained impressed by her safety features: "A ladder or escape is provided in each boiler room, engine room, and similar watertight compartment in order that the closing of the doors at any time shall not imprison the men working inside, but the risk of this happening is lessened by electric bells placed in the vicinity of each door, which ring prior to their closing and thus give warning to those below."

"The nerve system of the ship"
For a ship of that era, the *Titanic* relied heavily on electricity, which was still considered something of a

luxury. Four 400-kilowatt, steam-powered generators with dynamos produced electric current for the 150 electric motors aboard (76 of which drove the ventilation fans) and hundreds of miles of cables and wires supplied devices such as the 50-line internal telephone exchange, the 10,000 incandescent lamps, the 48 clocks and the 1,500 bell-pushes used to summon stewards. The main generating plant had a collective output of 16,000 amperes at 100 volts, bigger than the central stations of many large cities of the time.

The Shipbuilder enthused: "Electricity, it need hardly be pointed out, is extensively employed in all the departments of the *Olympic* and *Titanic*. In addition to the large supply required for lighting purposes, electrical power is used for deck cranes; cargo, boat and engine-room winches; passenger elevators; stores, mail and pantry lifts; ventilating and stokehold fans; cabin fans; motors for the cylinder-lifting gear; turbine-turning and lifting gear, and condenser sluice valves; the workshop machine tools; conveyor for marconigrams; gymnastic apparatus; kitchen and pantry machinery, such as the ice-rocker, dough-mixers, potato-peelers, roasters, knife-cleaners, mincers, hot plates, and electric irons; electric heaters; electric baths; main steam whistles; sounding machines; stoking indicators; boiler-room telegraphs; clocks; watertight doors; helm indicator; illuminated pictures; chimes; bells; loud-speaking and service telephones; submarine signaling; and wireless telegraphy. The electrical installation, therefore, may virtually be termed the nerve system of the ship."

There were 520 electric heaters on each ship and the first-class staterooms were equipped with fitted sockets for portable electric lamps or fans. *The Shipbuilder* noted: "Special dimming lamps with two filaments are also provided so that a light of small candle-power can be kept burning through the night, a feature which will appeal to nervous passengers." There were to be plenty of those.

It continued: "Emergency lamps on distinct circuits, deriving currents from the emergency dynamos, are placed at intervals in all the passages, public rooms, and compartments throughout the vessel, so that, in the unlikely event of an entire extinction of the ordinary lighting, there would still be illumination available at all the points where the passengers and crew would congregate. In fact, anyone could find their way from one end of the vessel to the other at night by means of the lights on these circuits."

A series of electrically illuminated signs were distributed throughout the first- and second-class accommodation to direct passengers to the main entrances and public rooms.

The Marconi wireless installation for telegraphy was another important safety feature. It was particularly powerful, guaranteeing a range of at least 350 miles. The apparatus was situated in a wireless house on the boat deck and was connected to a double aerial linked to the two masts, 205 feet above the sea. In case of a power failure, it had three separate supply sources — one from the electric light plant in the engine room, another situated elsewhere in the event of the engine room being flooded and a third from storage batteries in the operating room.

Each ship had eight electric cargo cranes, six with a capacity of $2\frac{1}{2}$ tons each, the other two of $1\frac{1}{2}$ tons each, plus four 3-ton electric cargo winches and four 15-cwt boat-hoisting winches.

The ships' whistles were also electrically

SAFETY MESSAGE
White Star made much of the **Titanic's** *safety features, which included the latest in wireless telegraphy.*

operated and, almost inevitably, were the largest in the world at the time. To sound a blast, the officer on the bridge simply had to close a switch. There was also an electric time-control arrangement whereby the whistles were blown automatically for eight to ten seconds every minute in thick fog.

Refrigeration equipment

The refrigeration installation was also modern and powered by two refrigeration engines situated in the port engine-room. The extensive provision rooms included separate cold chambers for beef, mutton, poultry and game, fish, vegetables, fruit, milk and butter, bacon and cheese, flowers, mineral waters, wines and spirits, and, perhaps most important of all given the type of passenger the liners hoped to attract, champagne. A large insulated compartment for the carriage of perishable cargo was placed next to the provision stores. The installation also consisted of a number of cold larders in the bars and pantries in different parts of the ship, plus arrangements for making ice and cooling the drinking water, which was available at various points in the first-, second- and third-class accommodation.

Mighty anchor

Naturally, a ship the size of the *Titanic* needed a special anchor to assist mooring. The usual arrangement was to have two bower anchors, but the builders realized the *Olympic* and the *Titanic* were so big that they would require an additional center anchor. It weighed 15½ tons and needed a team of 20 horses to deliver it. The side anchors each weighed half that amount. The cables used on the side anchors weighed 96 tons.

Lessons unheeded

The *Olympic* and the *Titanic* seemed to be shipbuilding masterpieces, triumphs of modern technology. *The Shipbuilder* remarked that "the design and construction of these two magnificent ships would have been beyond the range of possibility but for the cumulative experience available from earlier efforts during the past half-century."

Nobody foresaw that an iceberg might "slice the Titanic *down the side like a bloody great tin-opener."*

☆

Yet it appears that their designers failed to heed the lesson from previous transatlantic misadventures. In 1879, the Guion Line's *Arizona* had become shrouded in the fog that hung over the Newfoundland Grand Banks. With visibility severely restricted, she plowed into a 60-foot-high iceberg. Although her bows were crushed to pieces, she was able to make it back to St. John's, traveling stern-first. She had been saved from sinking by her collision bulkhead up front. Seven years later, the Cunarder *Oregon* was rammed amidships by a schooner off Fire Island, near New York. The 824 passengers and crew were taken off safely by another ship, but the *Oregon* sank.

The designers of the *Titanic* made little attempt to guard her most vulnerable area — her flanks. Instead, perhaps placing too much store in the good

THE *ARIZONA*
This ship struck an iceberg and survived, though the designers of White Star's great liners may have drawn false comfort from the fact.

fortune of the *Arizona*, they concentrated their defenses on the transverse bulkheads. They boasted that the ship would remain afloat even if two of the supposedly watertight compartments were flooded. Nobody foresaw that more than two of them might become flooded, or that an iceberg might (in the words of a shipping expert) "slice the *Titanic* down the side like a bloody great tin-opener." Nor did anyone consider that unless, as today's regulations require, the bulkheads extended upwards to a higher continuous deck, the inrush of water might flood one compartment, surge over the top and flood the one next door.

The giants emerge

In the meantime, confident that they were constructing the safest ships imaginable, the workers forged ahead — despite initial misgivings from the Catholic workforce when they read the anti-papal connotations in the builder's hull number 3909 04 on the *Titanic* (see page 8). Harland & Wolff management were obliged to reassure a delegation of workers that no insult was intended, the number was just a coincidence. Work resumed, but many considered the liner doomed.

Another bizarre rumor that spread around the yard was that the *Titanic* was being built at such a frenetic pace that some workers had been trapped inside her hull. Not surprisingly, this too was thought to be bad luck, not least for those inside. In spite of these superstitions, the construction was relatively uneventful. Records reveal that only two workers were killed in the period from keel laying to launch. This was considerably fewer than the unwritten rule of "one death for every £100,000 spent," which operated in the shipyards at the time.

The people of Belfast grew accustomed to the shells of the twin giants, which rose 100 feet above the Harland & Wolff slipways. Excitement mounted with the launch of the *Olympic* into the River Lagan on October 20, 1910, an operation supervised by Lord Pirrie in the presence of the Lord Lieutenant of Ireland, the Countess of Aberdeen and assembled dignitaries. As the *Olympic* set off, a sudden gust of wind blew her against the dry-dock, which dented some of her exterior plates. It was a clear warning of the problems of moving the biggest ship in the world in such a confined area. While the *Olympic* returned to dry-dock awaiting completion, work continued apace on her sister ship in the adjoining berth. Much of the heavy work on both ships was done by Harland & Wolff's 200-ton floating crane, one of the largest in the world at that time. The crane was capable of lifting a weight of 150 tons to a height of 149 feet, at a radius of 100 feet, with a list of only four degrees. This made it ideal for inserting heavyweight items such as the ships' boilers.

Outdated lifeboat regulations

The provision of enough lifeboats would turn out to be one of the most contentious issues in the wake of the *Titanic* disaster. The hopelessly outdated regulations of the British Board of Trade had not been amended since 1894, when the largest vessel afloat was the 12,950-ton *Campania* from Cunard. So no allowance had been made for the massive increase in ship size in recent years. Under the regulations, all British vessels of more than 10,000 tons had to carry 16 lifeboats with a capacity of 5,500 cubic feet, plus sufficient rafts and floats for 75 per cent of the capacity of the lifeboats. Consequently, a ship of 46,000 tons such as the *Titanic* was not required by law to carry any more lifeboats than one of 10,000 tons, even though it would undoubtedly be carrying many more passengers and crew. These regulations meant the *Titanic* had to carry boats for only 962 people when she had a capacity for 3,547.

Clearly it was a ridiculous and potentially deadly situation.

It is significant that at the planning stage, between four and five hours were devoted to discussing decor and fittings, but no more than 10 minutes was given over to lifeboat capacity. To his credit, Alexander Carlisle apparently had misgivings about the regulations. German and American rules already required a greater proportion of lifeboats than Britain, and Carlisle's original plan incorporated 64 boats, sufficient for everyone. But as discussions proceeded between builders and owners, Carlisle was obliged to modify the numbers first to 40, then 32 and finally to 16 30-foot-long boats, plus four Englehardt collapsible boats. It seemed that the money men preferred to utilize the deck space, which boats would take up, for larger promenades. In a tragic case of mistaken priorities, this was all part of the mission to provide the ultimate in luxury shipping.

The rules stipulated that *Titanic* had to carry boats for 962 people and her 16 lifeboats comfortably met the requirements with a seating capacity of 980. And White Star was proud that its designers had added the four collapsibles, with seating for 196 people, to raise the seating capacity to 1,176, well in excess of official needs. Even so, this represented only 53 per cent of the 2,207 people on board at the time of the disaster and only 30 per cent of the ship's total capacity.

Each pair of manually operated Welin davits was capable of lowering three boats in succession and could have been adapted to increase this number to four. Eight pairs of davits were fitted on either side of the ship, the foremost on each side being permanently swung out and carrying an emergency cutter that doubled as a lifeboat. A and B collapsibles were stowed on either side of the roof of the officers' house; C and D were placed one each side at the forward end of the officers' promenade on the boat deck. To make them easy to stow, the collapsibles had shallow wooden bottoms and canvas sides. Ironically, the Welin Davit and Engineering Co. Ltd. of London made a lot of the fact that they had

LOWERING THE LIFEBOATS
The **Titanic's** *Welin davits could lower three boats in succession. Originally enough boats were planned to evacuate all on board. By the time the* **Titanic** *went into service, there were lifeboat places for less than one in three.*

supplied the *Titanic* and took out advertisements in the run-up to the launch.

The *Olympic* was completed by the end of May 1911, just seven months after her launch. This was no mean achievement considering that Harland & Wolff was working simultaneously on two other White Star tenders (*Nomadic* and *Traffic*) for use at Cherbourg, the P&O liner *Maloja* (the largest ship of that fleet), the Aberdeen liner *Demosthenes* and the Union-Castle intermediate liner *Galway Castle*, as well as preparing for the launch of the *Titanic*. Out of the yard's work force of 14,000, up to 4,000 worked on the *Titanic*.

The *Titanic* was fully framed on April 6, 1910, a year after the keel had been laid. Plating was completed by October 19, 1910. On May 2, 1911, the *Olympic* underwent her trials in the fitting-out basin and her mighty engines turned for the first time. If there was any apprehension among the Harland & Wolff hierarchy, it quickly evaporated as the preliminary test proved satisfactory. Later in the month, before leaving for her trials at sea, the *Olympic* was opened to the public for five hours. Thousands of people paid 5s — a day's wages for many (Harland & Wolff workers were paid £2 for a 49-hour week) — to look over the magnificent new liner, although admission prices in the afternoon were generously reduced to 2s. And it was all in a good cause, with proceeds going to local Belfast hospitals.

On the morning of May 29, 1911, the *Olympic*, fueled by 3,000 tons of best Welsh coal and assisted by five tugs, headed off for two days of sea trials on Belfast Lough. She was accompanied by the new White Star tenders *Nomadic* and *Traffic* and, although the results of the tests were not made public, the engineering press cautiously reported that she had exceeded the designed speed of 21 knots by three-quarters of a knot. The Board of Trade was certainly satisfied with her performance and its Belfast surveyor, Francis Carruthers, promptly issued a certificate of seaworthiness valid for one year. R.M.S. *Olympic* could now enter service.

These were exciting times for the city of Belfast. On May 31, 1911, while the *Olympic* was completing her sea trials, crowds were assembling for the eagerly awaited launch of the *Titanic*. The day was clear and mild and, from early morning, yard workers and their families milled around the area alongside the River Lagan, eager to obtain a good vantage point. In many cases, this necessitated scaling walls, stacks of coal or timber and anything else that could be climbed. The important factor for them was that the view was free, for while the day was a holiday for Harland & Wolff workers, it was not a paid holiday.

White Star had invited the press and a party of dignitaries over for the launch and these were transported across the Irish Sea from Fleetwood in Lancashire by the specially chartered steamer *Duke of Argyll*. To accommodate the guests, three stands — admission to which was by invitation only — were erected in the yard close to the *Titanic* itself. Among them was J. Pierpont Morgan, effectively the owner of the *Titanic*, who had traveled from the United States specially for the occasion. As the *Duke of Argyll* approached Belfast at around 7:30AM, those on board got a splendid view of the *Titanic*'s sister ship as she lay in the Lough.

The city was a hive of activity. A ferry charged 2s for a cruise past the *Olympic* in Belfast Lough and promised to get passengers back in time for the launch of the *Titanic*. The Belfast Harbor Commissioners fenced off the section of the Albert Quay with the best view of proceedings and charged a few shillings for entry. All proceeds went to city hospitals. By 11:00AM, special trams were rumbling down Corporation Street towards the waterfront and shortly afterwards, the railway steamer *Slieve Bearnagh* departed from the Queen's Bridge jetty with another load of sightseers. As launch time approached, the stands, draped with bunting, were full to capacity and the banks of the Lagan lined with spectators. Estimates put the crowds present at more than 100,000, a third of the city's population. Belfast had never seen anything like it.

"There she goes!"

Shortly before noon, Lord Pirrie started receiving his distinguished guests at the shipyard's main offices on Queen's Road. Promptly at noon, he led the guests to the nearby observation stands, which afforded a splendid view of slip No. 3, where the hull of the *Titanic* shone with a fresh coat of black paint. Along the top of the gantry flew three flags — the Stars and Stripes, the Union Jack, and, in the middle, the big red company pennant with its five-pointed white star. Below flew a row of signal flags that spelt out GOOD LUCK. To facilitate the ship's passage, her slipway had been covered in 22 tons of soap and tallow, spread an inch thick.

With everyone sitting comfortably, Lord Pirrie,

wearing a jaunty yachting cap, inspected the launching gear for the final time. It was a big day for him. Not only did it mark the launch of his latest mammoth liner, but it was both his and Lady Pirrie's birthdays.

At 12:05PM, a red signal flag was hoisted on the sternpost of the *Titanic* to warn tugs and other small craft to keep clear. At 12:10PM, a red rocket was fired. This was the five-minute signal.

At 12:14PM, a second rocket soared into the blue sky. There was a hush of anticipation as Lord Pirrie conveyed his instructions to the launch foreman. As the last of the timber supports was knocked away, the ship stood motionless for what seemed like an eternity before a mighty cheer erupted, followed by a cry of "There she goes!" The soap and tallow had done the trick and *Titanic* slid slowly into the water at 12:15:02. There had been no official naming of the ship, no champagne ceremony. A shipyard worker explained the White Star philosophy to an inquiring visitor: "They just builds 'er and shoves 'er in."

The ship reached a speed of 12 knots before the hull was pulled up and held in place by special anchors, which had been embedded in the riverbed. These anchors were connected by seven-inch steel wire hawsers to eye-plates riveted to the hull plating. After the crowds had been allowed to soak up the awesome sight, the hull was detached from its restraining anchors and towed to its berth by five Liverpool tugs.

The Olympic enters service

As the crowds began to disperse, Lord and Lady Pirrie hosted a lunch for distinguished guests in the Harland & Wolff boardroom. Lesser guests (port officials, engineers, and naval architects) and the 90 members of the press were served a lunch of filet de boeuf washed down with Chateau Larose 1888 at Belfast's Grand Central Hotel, after which they were addressed by representatives of Harland & Wolff and White Star. At 2:30PM, the tender *Nomadic* left the quay, carrying a select band of guests (representatives of the owners and builders) out to the *Olympic*. Among those on board were the big three — J. Pierpont Morgan, J. Bruce Ismay and Lord Pirrie. At around 4:30PM, the *Olympic* and her distinguished party left Belfast bound for Liverpool, her port of registry and the city where White Star had its headquarters. She arrived off the Mersey the following day and, at Ismay's request, was again thrown open to the public before setting off for pastures new — her maiden voyage from Southampton to New York via Cherbourg in France and Queenstown (now Cobh) on the southern coast of Ireland.

Captain Edward John Smith

The *Olympic* left Southampton on June 14 with a full complement of passengers and the trip was uneventful apart from a minor scrape on her arrival in New York seven days later, when she almost sank the tug *O. L. Hallenbeck* under her stern. The captain was Edward John Smith, a man with more than 40 years' experience at sea. An avuncular man with a gray beard and barrel chest, he was the epitome of an old sea dog. He may have looked fearsome, but in truth he was soft-spoken, gentle and a leader in whom passengers and crews had great confidence. Over the years, White Star had built up a clientele of passengers who would not dream of crossing the Atlantic on a liner commanded by anyone other than Captain Smith.

He began his career as an apprentice on a clipper ship in 1869, before joining the White Star line in 1880 as fourth officer on the *Celtic*. He continued to work his way steadily up the ladder

PUNCTUAL START
The Titanic's launch was efficient but unceremonious. The ship hit the water for the first time at 12:15:02. Latecomers would have been disappointed.

Launch
OF
White Star Royal Mail Triple-Screw Steamer
"TITANIC"
At BELFAST,
Wednesday, 31st May, 1911, at 12-15 p.m.
Admit Bearer.

OFFICERS OF THE
OLYMPIC
Captain Edward
John Smith, later to
***command the* Titanic,**
is on the far right.
Lieutenant Murdoch
is on the far left.

and by 1887, he was appointed captain of the *Republic*. He went on to command 17 more White Star vessels. Among them was the maiden voyage of the *Adriatic* in 1907. Having brought her safely to New York, he told the press, "When anyone asks me how I can best describe my experiences of nearly 40 years at sea, I merely say 'uneventful.' I have never been in an accident of any sort worth speaking about. I never saw a wreck and have never been wrecked, nor was I ever in any predicament that threatened to end in disaster of any sort ... I cannot imagine any condition which would cause a ship to founder. I cannot conceive of any vital disaster happening to this vessel. Modern shipbuilding has gone beyond that."

In view of his outstanding safety record, it was highly appropriate that Captain Smith should be put in command of the *Olympic*, even though she was nearly twice as big as any ship he had previously handled. The incident at New York was therefore written off as a minor scrape, although the tug's owner did sue White Star for $10,000, prompting a countersuit from the company. Ultimately, both cases were dropped because of lack of evidence.

In the course of the summer and fall of 1911, work on fitting out *Titanic* continued and she gradually came to look more like the finished article. The electrical cables and air ducts were fitted, the deckhouses completed and the tiles for the swimming pool were laid. On September 18, White Star announced the date of the *Titanic*'s maiden voyage. It would be March 20, 1912. But within two days, the plans had to be changed — Captain Smith's luck had begun to run out.

Collision in the Solent

On that day, September 20, the *Olympic* set sail from Southampton on her fifth voyage to New York. She was under Smith's command, with the experienced George Bowyer as pilot. Shortly after noon, she approached Spithead off the Isle of Wight at the same time as the Royal Navy cruiser H.M.S. *Hawke* was sailing up the Solent towards Portsmouth at about 15 knots, having completed routine engine tests. The two vessels were thus heading in roughly the same direction on parallel courses. The *Olympic,* which was more than eight times the weight of the *Hawke,* slowed from 18 knots to about 11 and, with two blasts from her whistle, turned south of the Bramble sand bank and its treacherous waters.

By now, the *Hawke* was only 200 yards off the *Olympic*'s starboard side. As the two ships grew alarmingly nearer to each other, the cruiser seemed about to overtake the great liner, but as the latter picked up speed again, the *Hawke* dropped back. Suddenly, and without warning, the cruiser veered hard to port, heading straight for the *Olympic*. It later transpired that the wheel of the *Hawke* had jammed as her crew had attempted to rectify a wrong turn. Before they could do anything about it, currents created by *Olympic*'s massive hull were drawing their ship into the liner's starboard quarter. At 12:46PM, the cruiser rammed the *Olympic*'s hull with a tremendous thud. The collision left the *Hawke* with a badly crumpled bow, but she was able to limp to Portsmouth under her own power. However, the *Olympic* received a double gash towards the stern, which flooded two compartments, and damage to her starboard propeller. Her disappointed passengers were taken off by tender and she hobbled back to Southampton, where she was patched up before returning for full repairs to Belfast, which was the only dock large enough to accommodate her.

Initially, it seemed the *Hawke* was to blame for the accident, but the subsequent naval inquiry ruled otherwise and laid the guilt firmly with the *Olympic*. When the case went to court, the verdict was the same — that the 7,500-ton *Hawke* had been helplessly drawn into the side of the 45,000-ton *Olympic* by hydrodynamic forces beyond her control. Experts explained that when a ship's hull is moving forward, it pushes out a large amount of water on either side. This displaced water then surges back towards the stern and into the wake of the ship, in the process sucking in any smaller vessel in the immediate vicinity. In the end, the judgment was that "the collision was solely due to the faulty navigation of the *Olympic*." Captain Smith was exonerated — after all, George Bowyer was the pilot — in fact, he was rewarded for his hitherto exemplary career when he was promised command of the bigger and better *Titanic*, which was to be the White Star fleet's flagship.

The *Olympic* spent six weeks laid up at Belfast and her repairs assumed priority over fitting out the *Titanic*. It soon became apparent that White Star would have to put back the date of the *Titanic*'s maiden voyage, so a new date was announced — Wednesday, April 10, 1912.

The envy of the world

Throughout the winter, as the date of *Titanic*'s maiden voyage drew ever nearer, all manner of companies who had supplied equipment or goods to her began taking out advertisements in newspapers and trade periodicals. Aside from the davits, there was Wilson's Cooking Apparatus of Liverpool, Waygood Lifts, the Sunderland Forge and Engineering Co. Ltd. (supplier of winches), Hoskins & Sewell of Birmingham (berths, fittings, and mattresses), Bullivant & Co. Ltd. of London (wire rope makers), Allen & Simmonds Ltd. of Reading (suppliers of piston packings to *Olympic* and *Titanic*), William McGeoch & Co. Ltd. of Glasgow (specialists in stateroom furnishings, locks, lamps, and electric fittings), N. Burt & Co. Ltd. of London (supplier of door furnishings to the *Titanic*) and Ross-Schofield Marine Boiler Circulators. The latter's advertising copy, which said, "the new White Star liner *Titanic*, the largest vessel afloat, is fitted throughout all the boilers with Ross-Schofield Marine Circulators," may not have been the catchiest around, but it was effective.

Vinolia Otto Toilet Soap joined in the advertising rush, proclaiming that it was provided on board the *Titanic* for first-class passengers, thereby "offering a higher standard of toilet luxury and comfort at sea." It seemed everyone wanted to be associated with the *Titanic* and to bask in her reflected glory. Alas, some of these adverts were still appearing on April 16, 1912, the day after the disaster.

By the end of January, her funnels were in position and everything was on schedule for the April crossing to New York. But White Star wanted more than just a replica of the *Olympic* and, as the result of experience gained from the older sister, decided to incorporate a few design alterations to the *Titanic*, giving her a definite identity of her own. These changes to the passenger accommodation would make the *Titanic* even more luxurious and would also make her the biggest ship in the world.

"A HIGHER STANDARD OF TOILET LUXURY"
To manufacturers seeking endorsement, being a supplier to the **Titanic** *seemed the ultimate accolade.*

The principal exterior alteration was the addition of a glass canopy with sliding windows along the front section of promenade deck A to protect the passengers from inclement weather. This, plus changes to the sizes of the deckhouses, increased the tonnage of the *Titanic* from 45,000 to 46,328, making her heavier than the *Olympic*. The *Titanic* was now in a league of her own.

A tight timetable

Her sea trials were due to take place in Belfast Lough on April 1, but strong winds postponed them for 24 hours. The next day was fine and clear as 41 officers and senior crewmen (such as stewards, cooks, and engineers), plus 78 stokers and trimmers, boarded the *Titanic* under the command of Captain Smith. This was less than half of her full crew. Lord Pirrie was absent because of illness and was represented by Thomas Andrews, now managing director of the yard, and Edward Wilding, the senior naval architect. J. Bruce Ismay was also otherwise engaged and his place was taken by White Star director Harold Sanderson. The absence of such key personnel scarcely seemed to matter since the trials were viewed as purely academic.

Even at the unearthly hour of 6:00AM, crowds of spectators lined the bank of the Victoria Channel as *Titanic*, pulled by five tugs, slid away from her dock and headed off towards Belfast Lough. There, some two miles from the town of Carrickfergus, the liner was put through her paces. Her engines had been turned before in the course of fitting out, but not to move the ship. As steam was fed into the engines and smoke billowed from the funnels, *Titanic* moved for the first time under her own power.

The trials lasted just 12 hours and consisted of various routine maneuvers — stopping, starting, and stopping again, turning in circles at different speeds, and veering quickly from side to side in a slalomlike motion, to test her handling ability. Over lunch in the first-class dining-room, Francis Carruthers of the Board of Trade discussed the ship's performance to date with senior officers and engineers. Everyone was impressed with what they had seen.

In the afternoon came the emergency stop test. At a speed of 20 knots, the *Titanic* took 850 yards — just under half a mile — to come to a complete halt. Then it was time for the two-hour test over a straight course. For this, the crew took the liner to the mouth of the Lough and into the open waters of the Irish Sea. She proceeded to travel some 40 miles south before turning to head back to the Lough. Over those runs, she averaged a modest 18 knots, briefly touching 21 knots. But nobody was downhearted — the *Titanic* was about luxury rather than speed.

While the remainder of the crew were monitoring her performance, the two wireless operators, Jack Phillips and his junior Harold Bride (both Marconi employees, although classified on board ship as junior officers) were testing the ship's Marconi equipment. This too passed with flying colors.

Back in the Lough, the sun began to set on the magnificent spectacle that was the *Titanic*. Before the ship reached Belfast, Carruthers ordered one final test — the dropping and raising of the port and starboard anchors. When this was conducted satisfactorily, Carruthers duly signed the *Titanic*'s passenger certificate, that would be valid for one year. With the Board of Trade certificate having now been awarded, Andrews and Sanderson duly signed the papers that formally transferred the ship from builder to owner. Harland & Wolff had done their job. The *Titanic* was now officially the property of the White Star Line.

It had been hoped to put the *Titanic* on view to the mainland public at Liverpool, but the bad weather that delayed the trials for a day had put paid to that. For the new liner was on a strict schedule, which required her to be in Southampton for the midnight tide of April 3–4. So, after yard workers who were not needed for the 570-mile journey to Southampton were put ashore and fresh food

supplies and new chairs for the first-class reception room were taken aboard, the *Titanic* left Belfast shortly after 8:00PM. Her lights blazed brightly — she was like a beacon of optimism — as she steamed away into the night, off down the Lough towards the Irish Sea. She meant so much to the people of Belfast, yet the next time most of them would see her would be on the front pages of the world's newspapers.

All through the night, while the crew carried out minor adjustments, the largest ship afloat proceeded regally down the Irish Sea towards the Cornish coast. Alarmingly, on a brand-new ship, a fire broke out in the number 10 coal-bunker in number six boiler-room, directly below the third-class accommodation on E and F decks. Even more surprisingly, little attempt seemed to have been made to extinguish it, for the fire was still ablaze when, with more than 2,000 people on board, the liner sailed from Southampton on April 10. Perhaps it was only minor, but any fire on a ship is potentially catastrophic. However, the blaze failed to impede her progress on that first night at sea. At times on the journey to Southampton, she touched 23¼ knots and she was destined never to travel any faster.

Shortly after midday on April 3, she rounded Land's End and made her way up the English Channel. As darkness began to fall, she approached the Isle of Wight and the tricky navigational waters that had led to the temporary downfall of her sister ship. As she entered Southampton Water, she slowed down and the pilot came aboard to guide her along the last few miles. Finally, just before midnight, at high tide, she arrived at the newly constructed White Star Dock where she was met by five Red Funnel Line tugs. She came to rest at berth 44, with a six-day wait before she would sail off to New York — for the first, and last, time.

HAROLD BRIDE
Junior wireless operator. The wireless operators stayed at their posts until the bitter end.

Left
JACK PHILLIPS
Radio operator. He took a message from a westbound ship reporting pack ice and icebergs at the very spot where the **Titanic** *was to founder. This message never reached Captain Smith.*

CHAPTER TWO
THE GLITZ
AND THE
GLAMOR

Titanic **was the biggest and the best. And, of course, advertisements taken out by White Star gave an indication of her size and grandeur.**

FRESH AIR *Every class had its own promenade. The one for second-class was on the boat deck.*

The White Star line illustrated the *Titanic* in a vertical position (an unfortunate choice, given subsequent events), to show that at 882 ½ feet long, she compared favorably with many of the world's tallest buildings, such as New York's New Woolworth Building (750 feet high), its Metropolitan Tower (700 feet), the Washington Monument (555 feet) and Cologne Cathedral (516 feet). And her size was more than matched by her interior, which boasted the finest quality furnishings, carpet, and artwork. No expense was spared to make the *Titanic* the most luxurious vessel ever to have taken to the seas. By treating first-class ticket-holders as royalty, by creating second-class accommodation that could not fail to impress the most fastidious of passengers and by providing third-class amenities that would surpass those in other liners' second-class, White Star calculated that the public would not be able to resist the lure of the *Titanic*.

Strict segregation

The passenger accommodation was spread among the top seven decks, A to G, and was strictly segregated according to class with the most affluent housed on the upper levels. A descent into the bowels of the liner equated with a descent on the social ladder. The different classes ate in separate dining-rooms, read and talked in separate lounges, smoked in separate smoking-rooms, took the sea air on separate promenades, had their hair cut in separate barbers' shops and used different gangways to find

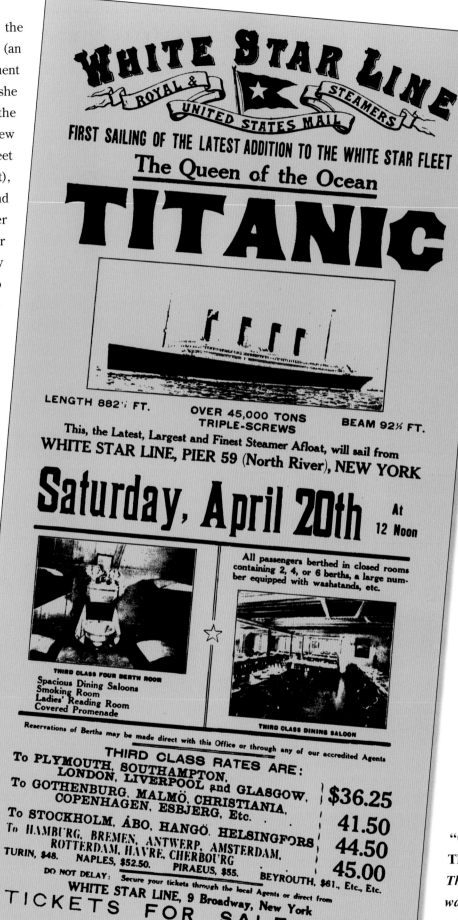

"QUEEN OF THE OCEAN" *The* **Titanic** *was billed as a nautical prodigy.*

their way around the ship. The long, wide passage that ran along the port side of E deck and was a popular route with the crew and steerage passengers, was nicknamed "Scotland Road" after the bustling, working-class thoroughfare in Liverpool, the *Titanic*'s port of registration. Meanwhile, a narrower passage on the starboard side of E deck, which was for first-class use, was known as "Park Lane" after the fashionable street in London's Mayfair. Virtually all the liner's most impressive facilities were solely for the use of first-class passengers.

"Unparalleled luxury"

All accommodation on A, B, and C decks was reserved for first-class passengers only. The finest were the staterooms, in particular the two parlor suites, located on either side of the forward grand entrance on C deck, and the two promenade suites that occupied a similar position on B deck. At £870, the promenade suites were the most expensive rooms on the *Titanic* and, according to *The Shipbuilder*, had been "fitted out with unparalleled luxury." The parlor and promenade suites each consisted of a sitting room, two bedrooms, two wardrobe rooms, and a private bath and lavatory, while the promenade suites also had their own private deck for taking the sea air. The sitting rooms were decorated in different styles and periods, including Louis Seize (XVI) and Louis Quatorze (XIV). Great attention was paid to detail. Many of the light fittings cost hundreds of pounds apiece and were wholly authentic to the period. And when booking the promenade suites, the occupant was given a free inside cabin for his or her servants — an offer too good to refuse.

Many of the other first-class staterooms were also decorated in styles of period grandeur — Italian Renaissance, Empire, Adams, Louis Quinze, Georgian, Regency, Queen Anne, Modern Dutch, and Old Dutch. All of the staterooms were linked by imposing long white corridors. Adjoining the parlor and promenade suites were six suites on each deck. Each of these comprised three combined bed-and-sitting-rooms with connecting doors, two wardrobe

rooms, plus private bath and lavatory. The rooms could be let separately if necessary. There was a wide variety of staterooms — one-, two- and three-berth — designed to cater for every taste. Some featured an adjoining cabin for one's personal servant. They boasted electric heaters, 4-foot-wide brass bedsteads, wicker armchairs, horsehair sofas, marble washstands, and fans in the ceiling. A green mesh net hung from the wall for the storage of valuables at night. Undoubtedly this was luxury of the highest order though many of the passengers had grown accustomed to it.

"A style peculiarly English"

All first-class accommodation was situated amidships. Access from one deck to another was either by two grand staircases (the main entrance was covered by a huge glass dome) or by three electric lifts that ran between E and A decks. As befitted a ship of her stature, the staircases on the *Titanic* were no ordinary staircases. They were decorated principally in late-seventeenth-century English style, but the heavily carved balustrade, with its wrought-iron scroll work, leaned more towards Louis XIV. The walls were covered in oak paneling.

The first-class dining saloon on D deck was the largest room on the *Titanic*, extending the entire width of the ship (92 feet), 114 feet in length and catering for more than 550 diners at one time (compared with the *Olympic*'s capacity of 532). It was modeled on the great Jacobean stately homes. A number of recessed bays enabled passengers to dine in privacy, while the lighting was designed so the whole room appeared to be bathed in permanent sunshine. The Captain's Table sat six and was positioned amidships at the forward end of this vast room. The official description of the saloon spared no adjective: "It is an immense room decorated in a style peculiarly English, reminiscent of early Jacobean times; but instead of the somber oak of the 16th and 17th centuries, it is painted a soft, rich white, which, with the coved and richly-molded ceilings and the spacious character of the apartment, would satisfy the most aesthetic critic. The furniture is of oak designed

The promenade suites had their own private deck for taking the sea air.

☆

to harmonize with its surroundings." Dining hours were one of the few events that were the same for all classes on the *Titanic*. Breakfast was served from 8:30AM to 10:30AM, lunch from 1:00PM to 2:30PM and dinner from 6:00PM to 7:30PM. However, certain first-class facilities, such as the restaurant, remained open longer.

Adjoining the dining saloon was a 54-foot-long reception room where first-class passengers gathered before dining. This also occupied the full width of the ship. The floor of the reception room was covered in a rich Axminster carpet and the furniture included sumptuous Chesterfields, cane chairs, and a grand piano.

Louis Seize elegance

The restaurant on B deck offered an extensive à la carte menu to first-class passengers, something that was not available in the dining saloon. Decorated in the style of Louis XVI and paneled from floor to ceiling in French walnut, it was a room of considerable beauty. Even the fastenings and hinges were faithful to the period. Tables sat between two and eight people, each of the 49 tables being lit by a crystal standard lamp and set with the finest silver and china. In the center of the 60-foot-long by 45-foot-wide room, crystal chandeliers hung from the floral-patterned plaster ceiling above a rose-colored carpet. Employing staff from Luigi Gatti's fashionable London restaurants, it seated 137 diners and was open from 8:00AM to 11:00PM daily. Passengers who opted to use the restaurant throughout the voyage, instead of the dining saloon, were given a rebate of between £3 and £5 on their tickets.

The reception room next to the first-class dining saloon on the *Olympic* proved so popular that for the *Titanic*, an additional reception room was provided, adjoining the restaurant. Decorated in Georgian style and littered with elegant settees and easy chairs upholstered in carmine silk, it was the perfect

THE GRAND STAIRCASE
Covered by a huge glass dome, richly decorated and luxuriously ornate, this impressive entrance introduced first-class passengers to **Titanic's** *world of opulent travel.*

ATTENTION TO DETAIL
Authentic reproduction furniture graced the sitting rooms of **Titanic's** *first-class parlor and promenade suites.*

PERIOD GRANDEUR
First-class staterooms also featured a range of classic styles.

Opposite
THE READING AND WRITING ROOM
A large bay window offered a superb view out to sea.

meeting place for friends and parties prior to taking their tables in the restaurant.

But the most startling innovation on B deck was the Café Parisien, a unique feature. Located on deck space outside the restaurant, it was to become a favorite haunt of younger passengers. It quickly attracted the attention of the *Southampton Times and Hampshire Advertiser* which on April 5, 1912, in their build-up to the maiden voyage, wrote: "The Café Parisien has the appearance of a charming sun-lit verandah tastefully arranged with trellis-work, and chairs in small groups surrounding convenient tables. It will also form a further addition to the restaurant, as lunches and dinners can be served with the same excellent service and all the advantages of the restaurant itself."

"Equal to the finest hotels on shore"

The first-class lounge on A deck was designed in the style of Louis XVI and based on the Palace at Versailles. At one end stood a large fireplace and at the other a bookcase from where passengers could borrow a selection of reading matter. A feature of the room was its height (12 feet 3 inches). Adjacent to the lounge was the reading and writing room, decorated entirely in white and from where a large bay window offered a superb view out to sea. Further along A deck was the Georgian smoking-room, paneled in finest mahogany inlaid with mother-of-pearl. Next to the smoking-room was the verandah café and palm court where passengers sipped after-dinner coffee and listened to chamber music. To create the illusion that the café was on shore, ivy and other climbing plants were trained up the green trellis-work panels. As *The Shipbuilder*

FIRST-CLASS FACILITIES

A vast range of facilities were open to first-class passengers — gymnasium, squash court, Turkish and electric baths, swimming pool, barber's shop, a dark room for photographers, a clothes-pressing room, a library, and a special dining room for maids and valets.

Situated on the boat deck, the gymnasium measured 44 feet long, 18 feet wide, and 9 feet 6 inches high. It had eight large windows and was adorned with illuminated, multicolored pictures of the *Titanic* and a map of the world showing the network of White Star steamship routes. Besides "obtaining beneficial exercise and endless amusement," passengers could tackle apparatus that simulated horse-riding, cycling, and rowing, all supervised by an instructor.

The Turkish baths, complete with shampooing rooms, were situated on F deck. The cooling room was decorated in seventeenth-century Arabian style. The portholes were "concealed by an elaborately carved Cairo curtain, through which the light fitfully reveals something of the grandeur of the mysterious East." The room had a mosaic floor, blue and green tiled walls, beautiful gilded beams, and a deep-red ceiling supported by stanchions encased in carved teak. Bronze Arab lamps were suspended from the walls, above low couches and inlaid Damascus coffee tables. To one side of the room stood a handsome marble drinking fountain, set in a frame of tiles. Passengers paid 4s to use the Turkish baths or the adjoining electric baths.

The swimming pool was on the starboard side of F deck. It measured 30 feet long and 14 feet wide and was furnished with the most up-to-date equipment. Use of the pool cost 1s.

G deck housed the squash court which, as *The Shipbuilder* noted, "should prove popular with those disposed to athletic exercise." Its height was such that it reached up into F deck. The court was 30 feet long and 20 feet wide and also featured a spectator gallery and a resident professional, Frederick Wright. The price for the court was 2s for half an hour.

The swimming pool

observed, "Everything has been done in regard to the furniture and fittings to make the first-class accommodation more than equal to that provided in the finest hotels on shore."

Second-class, first-rate

The 207 second-class cabins were positioned on D, E, F, and G decks, access between the decks being via the second-class grand staircase or by an electric lift that ran from G deck to the boat deck. The corridors were carpeted in red or green and the walls had oak panels. The second-class staterooms aboard the *Titanic* were the equal of first-class accommodation on practically any other ship of that era. The well-lit two-, three-, and four-berth cabins were fitted with mahogany furniture, which provided a sharp contrast to the white walls. The floors were covered in linoleum tiles.

THE GYMNASIUM
Here you were offered "beneficial exercise and endless amusement."

UPSTAIRS, DOWNSTAIRS

First-class passengers prepare for a North Atlantic promenade.

The cost of a first-class suite on the *Titanic* ranged from £400 to £870 for a one-way ticket. Those who had paid the top prices for the promenade suites on B deck were allowed access to adjoining private decks, 50 feet long, the walls of which were decorated in half-timbered, Elizabethan style. This was a feature unique to the *Titanic*.

Other first-class passengers could use the 500-foot-long enclosed promenades on A and B decks as well as a 200-foot-long open promenade on the boat deck. The cheapest first-class passage was £23 without meals.

At the other end of the scale, some third-class passengers shared up to ten in a cabin, and as many as 164 slept in dormitories way down on G deck. The cheapest third-class fare was £7 15s, including meals. The third-class promenade was a much humbler affair on C deck, although those in steerage were also allowed access to a large covered area on D deck, which was fitted with tables and chairs. The second-class promenades included a 145-foot-long area on the boat deck and a covered section 84 feet in length, with sliding windows at the side, on C deck next to the second-class library.

The second-class dining saloon was situated on D deck, close to its larger, first-class cousin. Measuring 71 feet in length and extending the full width of the ship, it had oak wall panels, long tables, and revolving chairs to provide seating for 394. The deck above housed the second-class library, a splendid room with sycamore paneling, mahogany furniture, a Wilton carpet, and a large bookcase. Immediately above the library, on B deck, was the second-class smoking-room, decorated in the style of the Louis XVI period. The furniture was oak, upholstered with plain dark green morocco leather. Second-class passengers also had use of a barber's shop on E deck.

The view from third class

The 222 third-class cabins were to be found on D, E, F, and G decks. The staterooms were surprisingly large and airy, while the pine wall paneling and impressive floor coverings represented a significant improvement on the bare metal walls and floors that had previously been the norm on most liners. Since the *Titanic* was not designed to carry large numbers of immigrants, there was just one area of open berths on G deck.

The third-class dining saloon on F deck was 100 feet long and seated 473. It was suitably basic, although the chairs made a refreshing change from the usual bolted-down benches. Third-class passengers were also allowed to use the general room — a simple affair with benches, tables, chairs, and a piano for singalongs — and a smoking-room with teak furniture. Next to the smoking-room was a bar. Another third-class bar was situated on D deck. The third-class accommodation was more than adequate, but there the pipes and girders were laid bare, rather than hidden behind paneling or tapestries as they were in first-class. Despite their avowed dedication to the comfort of all passengers, White Star evidently still harbored some reservations about the behavior of ordinary men and women. Accordingly, in third-class, all single men and women were quartered separately at opposite ends of the ship. Naturally no such restrictions applied in first or second-class. Also, while first-class passengers were able to enjoy the ship's facilities well into the night, White Star encouraged all third-class travelers to retire by 10:00PM.

WRITING HOME
First-class passenger Richard May rushed to mail a note with the **Titanic** *letterhead as a souvenir of his arrival on board.*

FIRST-CLASS STATEROOMS

Brass bedsteads, wicker armchairs, and marble washstands came with the specification.

Very few amenities were open to passengers of more than one class. One honorable exception was the ship's orchestra, which played for both first and second-class ears. Led by 33-year-old Wallace Hartley, an accomplished violinist recruited from the *Mauretania* (pianist Theodore Brailey and cellist Roger Bricoux were also wooed from another vessel — the *Carpathia*), the band had eight members and a repertoire of 352 tunes. The musicians were expected to know each tune by its number when the leader called for it to be played.

The group were divided into two sections. An immaculately attired trio on piano, violin, and cello performed in the second-class lounge and dining saloon and in the first-class reception room outside the à la carte restaurant and the Café Parisien. Meanwhile, the remaining quintet, with Hartley at the helm, played teatime and after-dinner concerts, as well as Sunday service.

The *Titanic* had a capacity of 2,603 passengers — 905 in first-class, 564 in second-class, and 1,134 in third-class — plus 944 crew members, for a total of 3,547. Of the crew, more than half tended to the whims of the passengers, 325 looked after the engines and the remaining 66, including the captain and his seven deck officers, sailed the ship. The captain's suite and the deck officers' cabins were on the boat deck near the officers' promenade. Mirroring the passenger accommodation, the lower-ranking crew members were housed further down the ship, between C and G decks. Similarly, the different divisions of crew — caterers and stewards, engineers, firemen — each had their own separate social rooms.

Passengers diverted

As April 10 approached, sightseers flocked to Southampton to glimpse the ship about which so

SEA FARE

The food on board the *Titanic* amply lived up to the ship's claim of providing everything that a top London or New York hotel could offer. The à la carte restaurant for first-class diners was every bit the equal of the Café Royal or Savoy Grill, featuring the finest in international food and wines. The first-class dining saloon was equally appetizing. For dinner on April 14 (the last supper for so many), the first-class menu offered a seven-course meal. It included various hors d'oeuvres or oysters; a choice of two soups; salmon; filet mignon, sauté of chicken Lyonnaise or stuffed marrow; lamb, duckling or sirloin of beef, plus vegetables; a choice of four light savory dishes such as cold asparagus vinaigrette and pâté de foie gras; and four desserts — Waldorf pudding, peaches in Chartreuse jelly; chocolate and vanilla eclairs and French ice cream.

On the same evening, second-class diners were presented with clear soup, a fish course of baked haddock, a choice of curried chicken with rice, spring lamb or roast turkey with vegetables or rice, a selection of desserts (plum pudding, wine jelly, coconut sandwich or American ice cream), nuts and fruit, cheese, biscuits, and coffee.

Whereas first- and second-class meals were referred to as "lunch" and "dinner," the principal meals in third-class were given the more down-market labels of "dinner" and "tea." Dinner was taken at midday, instead of in the evening. Naturally, the menus lacked the refinement of the two cabin classes and had a more limited choice, but they compensated for this with generous portions. Breakfast consisted of cereal, kippers or boiled egg, bread, marmalade, and tea or coffee. Dinner began with soup, followed by a meat dish such as roast pork, a cooked dessert, and fruit. Tea consisted of a cooked course, bread or buns, a light dessert, and tea. There was also a late supper of cheese and biscuits or gruel and coffee.

For speed of service, the first- and second-class kitchens, the serving rooms, pantries, and bakeries were situated on D deck between the respective dining saloons. The kitchens boasted two huge ranges, thought to be the largest in the world, each containing 19 ovens. In addition, there were four silver grills, two large roasters, steam ovens, and electrical slicing, potato-peeling, mincing, whisking, and freezing machines.

THE PANTRY

LARDER

Prior to leaving Southampton, the *Titanic* took delivery of the following foodstuffs:

Fresh meat	75,000 lb.	Sugar	10,000 lb.	Tomatoes	2¾ tons
Fresh fish	11,000 lb.	Cereals	10,000 lb.	Fresh asparagus	800 bundles
Salt and dried fish	4,000 lb.	Flour	200 barrels	Fresh green peas	2,250 lb.
Bacon and ham	7,500 lb.	Oranges	36,000	Onions	3,500 lb.
Poultry and game	25,000 lb.	Lemons	16,000	Potatoes	40 tons
Fresh eggs	40,000	Grapes	1,000 lb.	Jams and marmalade	1,120 lb.
Sausages	2,500 lb.	Fresh milk	1,500 gallons	Beer and stout	20,000 bottles
Sweetbreads	1,000	Fresh cream	1,200 qts.	Wines	1,500 bottles
Ice cream	1,750 qts.	Condensed milk	600 gallons	Spirits	850 bottles
Coffee	2,200 lb.	Fresh butter	6,000 lb.	Mineral waters	15,000 bottles
Tea	800 lb.	Grapefruit	50 boxes		
Rice, dried beans, etc.	10,000 lb.	Lettuce	7,000		

TABLEWARE

Vast quantities of crockery, cutlery and glassware were also delivered between April 4 and 10:

Breakfast cups	4,500	Breakfast saucers	4,500	Dinner forks	8,000
Tea cups	3,000	Tea saucers	3,000	Fruit forks	1,500
Coffee cups	1,500	Coffee saucers	1,500	Fish forks	1,500
Beef tea cups	3,000	Soufflé dishes	1,500	Oyster forks	1,000
Cream jugs	1,000	Wine glasses	2,000	Butter knives	400
Breakfast plates	2,500	Champagne glasses	1,500	Sugar tongs	400
Dessert plates	2,000	Cocktail glasses	1,500	Fruit knives	1,500
Soup plates	4,500	Liqueur glasses	1,200	Fish knives	1,500
Pie dishes	1,200	Claret jugs	300	Table and dessert knives	8,000
Beef tea dishes	3,000	Salt shakers	2,000	Dinner spoons	5,000
Cut glass tumblers	8,000	Salad bowls	500	Dessert spoons	3,000
Water bottles	2,500	Pudding dishes	1,200	Egg spoons	2,000
Crystal dishes	1,500	Sugar basins	400	Teaspoons	6,000
Celery glasses	300	Fruit dishes	400	Salt spoons	1,500
Flower vases	500	Finger bowls	1,000	Mustard spoons	1,500
Ice cream plates	5,500	Butter dishes	400	Toast racks	400
Dinner plates	12,000	Vegetable dishes	400	Nut crackers	300
Coffee pots	1,200	Entrée dishes	400	Asparagus tongs	400
Teapots	1,200	Meat dishes	400	Grape scissors	100

LINEN

The *Titanic*'s linen supply contained:

Aprons	4,000	Bed covers	3,600	Bath towels	7,500
Blankets	7,500	Eiderdown quilts	800	Fine towels	25,000
Table cloths	6,000	Single sheets	15,000	Lavatory towels	8,000
Glass cloths	2,000	Double sheets	3,000	Roller towels	3,500
Cooks' cloths	3,500	Pillow slips	15,000	Pantry towels	6,500
Counterpanes	3,000	Table napkins	45,000	Miscellaneous items	40,000

much fuss was being made. But White Star had a major headache. It had anticipated a huge demand for tickets from people wanting to be part of the maiden voyage of the world's largest liner, but applications came in a steady trickle rather than a flood. The result was that the company was facing the unpalatable prospect of its flagship departing on its much-hyped trip to New York barely half full. The reason for the apathy was largely attributable to a series of strikes throughout the spring of 1912 that had seriously damaged the shipping industry, particularly a six-week national coal strike that was not resolved until April 6. Voyages were canceled or postponed at the last minute, leaving passengers bewildered and disillusioned. In order to save face, White Star decided to divert passengers from other liners on to the *Titanic*.

Below capacity

Despite these measures, there were plenty of gaps, particularly in the first- and second-class sections, both of which were less than half full. When she headed out into the North Atlantic, the *Titanic* was believed to be carrying a total of 2,207 passengers and crew — more than 1,000 below capacity. There were 322 passengers in first-class, 275 in second-

FIRST-CLASS RECEPTION ROOM
Resplendent in its Axminster carpet, this was as wide as the ship itself.

COLONEL JOHN JACOB ASTOR IV

The man who chose as his second wife a woman younger than his son and scandalized New York society, was on board.

class, 712 in third-class, and an enlarged crew of 898. In view of what was to follow, it was merciful that White Star had not been able to fill every place. This would have been of little comfort, of course, to those passengers who had been diverted from other, safer liners.

Millionaires ...

What it lacked in quantity, the guest list made up for in quality, reading like a who's who of New York and Philadelphia society. The British well-to-do were generally unimpressed by the razzmatazz of maiden voyages and preferred to sail with the tried and trusted Cunarders, hence the first-class suites were dominated by Americans. Aside from a list of passengers calculated to be worth a total of $250 million, the ship's cargo also included a priceless jeweled copy of *The Rubáiyát of Omar Khayyám*. And no fewer than 20 newly-wed couples chose to take their honeymoon aboard the *Titanic*. Only one of these couples — the Bishops from Michigan — lived to tell the tale. The remainder of the brides were widowed by the disaster.

A glance through the passenger list reveals the well-known and controversial Colonel John Jacob Astor IV, whose personal wealth was estimated at $87 million. Inheriting the family fortune (his great-grandfather was a pioneering fur trader), Astor had proceeded to expand it with a succession of shrewd real estate investments that resulted in his ownership of a sizable chunk of Manhattan. Like a number of his

MADELEINE ASTOR

The Astors' second honeymoon was cut short when she found out she was pregnant. She boarded the ship with her husband.

contemporaries, Astor had little concept of poverty: he once proclaimed, "A man who has a million dollars is as well off as if he were rich." He also had a passion for modes of transport. He invented a brake for bicycles, a pneumatic device for flattening road surfaces, and was also fined by a British court for exceeding the speed limit in his motor car. On another occasion, he had disappeared for 16 days in the Caribbean aboard his private yacht, causing national concern as the money markets began to stutter.

But at 46, the recently divorced millionaire had scandalized New York society by choosing as his second wife an 18-year-old woman, Madeleine Force, who was younger than his son Vincent. They married in September 1911 and decided to escape the wagging tongues and press intrusion by taking a long second honeymoon in Egypt and Paris. Then, on learning that Madeleine was five months' pregnant, they chose to head back to New York and booked a place on the *Titanic*. Together with their entourage, which included his manservant, her maid, and a nurse, they occupied C62, one of the luxurious parlor suites.

Magnates ...

The second parlor suite (C55) was occupied by an elderly couple who were to become part of *Titanic* folklore — Isidor and Ida Straus. Arriving in the United States shortly before the American Civil War, Straus became a salesman for Confederate bonds, before starting up a small china business in Philadelphia. He was quick to spot the business potential of a blossoming store in New York, Macy's, and asked whether he and his brother could sell glass and chinaware there, in return for which they would give Macy's 10 per cent of their sales. Within 10 years, the brothers Straus owned the whole store. By 1912, Isidor Straus was slowing down, devoting less time to business and more to charitable work. In their twilight years, he and his wife also had time at last to enjoy hobbies and traveling. They had been on holiday in the spring of that year and had decided that the perfect way to round things off was to journey home on the maiden voyage of the *Titanic*.

The Wideners of Philadelphia had made their money in banking and railroads. Representing them on board the *Titanic* were George Widener, his wife Eleanor, and their 27-year-old son Harry, a Harvard graduate who displayed a greater interest in books than in transport. The Wideners were seriously rich, with a personal wealth estimated at $30 million. Eleanor alone, for example, was traveling with a pearl necklace insured for $600,000 (or $4 million in today's money). George and Eleanor Widener were to host the last great dinner aboard the *Titanic*.

The Wideners were not the only railroad luminaries converging on Southampton. There was Charles M. Hays, the Canadian president of Grand Trunk Pacific Railroad, the company that had recently built a bridge over the Niagara River at Niagara Falls. And there was John B. Thayer, second vice president of the Pennsylvania Railroad Company.

Glitterati ...

Other notable passengers included the Countess of Rothes (on her way to join her fruit-farmer husband in Canada); Major Archibald Butt, military aide to US President William H. Taft; English journalist, editor, and spiritualist William T. Stead, who was America-bound to address a peace conference at the specific request of President Taft; the celebrated Broadway producer Henry B. Harris and his wife René; American artist Frank Millet; writer Jacques Futrelle; silent movie star Dorothy Gibson; Francis M. Warren, former senator for Wyoming; Dr. Washington Dodge, the Assessor for San Francisco; and historian Colonel Archibald Gracie, author of a book about the American Civil War, who was returning to his Washington home, having been in England conducting research into the war of 1812.

... and a new Renault car

Naturally, most of the first-class passengers carried a quantity of baggage in keeping with their status. Although Archie Butt was away from the White House less than six weeks, he needed seven trunks for his wardrobe. Mr. and Mrs. Arthur Ryerson (a steel magnate) topped that with 16 trunks. Wealthy Philadelphians Mrs. Charlotte Cardeza and her son Thomas (both of whom were to board the ship at Cherbourg, occupying promenade suite B51) brought with them 14 trunks, four suitcases, three crates, and a medicine chest. The contents included 70 dresses, 10 fur coats, 38 feather boas, 22 hatpins, and 91 pairs of gloves. Mrs. Cardeza did not believe in traveling light.

Another prominent Philadelphian, Billy Carter, came aboard with 60 shirts, 15 pairs of shoes, two sets of tails, 24 polo sticks ... and a new Renault car. Everything, including the car, went down with the *Titanic*. Fortunately, Carter survived.

Some passengers were accompanied by their dogs. Henry Sleeper Harper of the famous

ISIDOR STRAUS
The co-owner of Macy's and his wife were returning from a European vacation and occupied luxury suite C55.

SOME MISSED THE BOAT

At least 55 passengers canceled their bookings on the *Titanic* at very short notice. The most intriguing was J. Pierpont Morgan (citing ill health), but a former business associate of his, Robert Bacon, the outgoing American Ambassador to Paris, also backed out, shortly after receiving a phone call from Morgan. When canceling, Bacon claimed he had to stay on in Paris to smooth the way for his successor.

American steel baron Henry C. Frick had originally reserved luxury suite B52, but withdrew after his wife sprained her ankle on a cruise to Madeira. The suite was reallocated to Morgan and, when he excused himself, it was put in the name of Mr. and Mrs. J. Horace Harding. But they preferred to travel home on the faster *Mauretania*, leaving the most sought-after suite on the ship in the hands of J. Bruce Ismay.

Railroad and shipping boss George W. Vanderbilt canceled the booking for himself and his wife after her mother, Mrs. Dressler, had expressed grave reservations about maiden voyages. Her powers of persuasion were such that the Vanderbilts pulled out, even though their luggage had already been sent aboard. Their dutiful servant, second-class passenger Frederick Wheeler, agreed to travel with the luggage to America and went down with the *Titanic*.

Mr. and Mrs. James V. O'Brien had to abandon their plans to travel on board the *Titanic* when a lawsuit they had taken out in an Irish court ran longer than anticipated.

The Rev. J. Stuart Holden, rector of St. Paul's Church in London's Portman Square, withdrew on the eve of sailing because his wife was ill.

A Mr. M. Forster had booked a passage on the *Titanic* for himself and his niece, but decided to cancel and sail on the *Adriatic* instead. He said, "I was a little afraid of new machinery and that was one of the reasons I decided not to return from Europe on the *Titanic*."

Mr. and Mrs. Edward W. Bill of Philadelphia had been eagerly looking forward to sailing on the *Titanic* until, while staying at London's Hotel Cecil prior to setting off for Southampton, Mrs. Bill had a premonition of impending doom. The couple sailed instead on the *Mauretania* and, on safely reaching New York, Mr. Bill revealed, "I had our rooms all picked out on the *Titanic*, and I told my wife that it would be interesting to be on the greatest ship in the world on her maiden trip. Mrs. Bill was not very enthusiastic, and when I started for the White Star office to get the tickets, she begged me not to go. She said that she couldn't tell why, but said she didn't want to go on the *Titanic*. I had never known her to object to any plan of travel I suggested before, but this time she was immovably firm, and I yielded to her wishes reluctantly."

An unnamed Irish farmer had decided to emigrate to America and had booked his passage in the steerage section of *Titanic*. But his mother apparently dreamed on three successive nights that the ship would sink in mid-ocean, killing everyone on board. She told her son and begged him to stay at home. After much persuasion, he agreed and canceled the booking.

In addition to the passengers, 22 crew members who had "signed on" with the *Titanic* failed to make the maiden voyage. Three brothers from Southampton, Bertram, Tom, and Alfred Slade, who had been lined up as trimmers in the ship's coal-bunkers, had a lucky escape when they were prevented from boarding the liner in time by a passing train. Another Southampton man, Harry Burrows, had stayed at home for a month so he could get a job on the *Titanic*. On the morning of April 10, he duly said goodbye to his mother and headed down to the docks, only to return shortly afterwards, having had an amazing change of heart. He told his mother that "some sort of feeling" had come over him.

The 22 crew members who did not sail were: C. Blake; F. T. Bowman; B. Brewer; W. Burrows; J. Coffey; W. W. Dawes; P. Dawkins; P. Ettlinger; B. Fish; R. Fisher; A. Haveling; F. Holden; P. Kilford; A. Manley; W. J. Mewe; E. di Napoli; V. Penny; J. Shaw; W. Sims; A. Slade; D. Slade; Thos. Slade. They were replaced by: D. Black; J. Brown; W. Dickson; R. Dodds; A. Geer; T. Gordon; E. Hosgood; L. Kinsella; A. Locke; W. Lloyd; F. O'Connor; A. Windebank; H. Witt.

publishing family had his prize Pekinese, Sun Yat-sen; Robert W Daniel, a Philadelphia banker, was bringing back the champion French bulldog that he had just purchased in Britain; and John Jacob Astor was accompanied by his Airedale terrier, Kitty.

Nothing was too much trouble to please the first-class passengers. The 190 families in first-class were attended by a total of 23 handmaids, eight valets, plus assorted nurses and governesses. And if one did not have one's own personal servant on board, one could count on the ship's own network of stewards and stewardesses, all of whom, at the ring of a bell, would gladly perform chores such as laying out dinner suits and helping one dress for dinner. To ensure that these VIPs were not kept waiting for a second longer than was absolutely necessary, the stewards and stewardesses were housed nearby — in tiny cabins, holding up to four people, and tucked into corners of the spacious first-class corridors. There was never any danger of a steward forgetting his place.

In the midst of the assembled glitterati, there was one notable absentee. Suite number B52, the promenade suite opposite Mrs. Cardeza's, was to have been occupied by J. Pierpont Morgan, the ship's owner. But Morgan withdrew at the last minute, claiming that he was feeling unwell. Two days after the disaster, a reporter tracked down 75-year-old Morgan to the Grand Hotel in the French spa town of Aix-les-Bains, where the shipping magnate was found to be in perfectly good health and in the company of his French mistress. His late withdrawal from the voyage has been used by conspiracy theorists as a further indication that the *Titanic* was sunk deliberately. The suite, which had been designed to Morgan's own specifications, was taken instead by J. Bruce Ismay, along with his valet and secretary.

Busy preparations

The week between the *Titanic*'s arrival in Southampton and her departure for New York was one of great activity. Provisions, cargo and supplies were taken aboard, as was coal, gleaned from five other IMM ships in port, plus a quantity left behind by the *Olympic*, which had sailed for New York just hours before

THE COUNTESS OF ROTHES
She famously took the tiller on one of the lifeboats and also helped with the rowing.

A MOUNTAIN OF PAPERWORK
One of the supplies to be taken on board was a vast range of stationery.

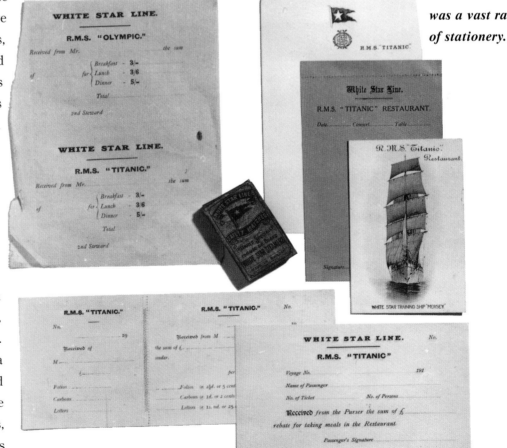

ON THE BRIDGE
Captain Smith (seated, left) and senior officers of the Titanic.

the *Titanic* docked at Southampton. But still the fire in one of the bunkers was allowed to burn unchecked.

The officers, under Captain Smith, had come aboard at Belfast for the sea trials, with the apparent exception of the man who was to become chief officer, Henry T. Wilde. Transferred from the *Olympic* because of his knowledge of these new mammoth liners, Wilde's switch caused a late

readjustment in the senior ranks of the *Titanic*. The previous chief officer, William M. Murdoch, became first officer; Charles H. Lightoller moved from first to second; Herbert J. Pitman (third), Joseph G. Boxhall (fourth), Harold G. Lowe (fifth) and James P. Moody (sixth) remained unaltered, but the former second officer, David Blair, left the ship altogether.

Most of the crew were signed on in the course of

Saturday, April 6. There was no shortage of volunteers, with people desperate to find work again following their enforced lay-off caused by the coal strike. Consequently, the hiring halls were packed to the rafters, mainly with local working-class men from Southampton, although others traveled from as far afield as Belfast, Liverpool, Dublin and London, all excited at the prospect of sailing on the world's newest and finest ship.

Among those who signed on that day as a fireman was a Thomas Hart from 51 College Street, Southampton. Having produced the necessary Certificate of Continuous Discharge paybook in that name, the man took his place on the *Titanic* and duly went down with her. Hart's elderly mother wept uncontrollably at her loss, but was even more stunned when her embarrassed son returned home a month later in perfect health. It transpired that the real Hart had been drunk in a pub and had lost his discharge book. An unknown impostor had seized the opportunity to take his job and had paid for his chicanery with his life.

"Ship loaded and ready for sea"

The morning of Wednesday, April 10, 1912 was bright and breezy. A sense of tremendous expectation hung in the cool spring air. The general crew reported to the dockyard at 6:00AM and were directed to their quarters on board ship. Half an hour later, Thomas Andrews, Harland & Wolff's official representative on the voyage, boarded the ship. He had spent the previous week examining every aspect of the ship in great detail, making copious notes on any minor improvements that could be incorporated into the design to make the *Titanic* more magnificent. Captain Smith arrived by taxi at 7:30AM and at 8:00AM the Blue Ensign was run up at the stern. While the crew reported on deck for muster, Captain Maurice Clarke of the Board of Trade carried out the final inspection of the ship. He paid considerable attention to the lifeboats, ensuring that they were in proper working order, but failed to spot the fire down in bunker number 10. Satisfied that all was well and that with 5,892 tons of coal the *Titanic* was carrying

enough fuel to reach New York, Clarke signed the ship's papers. Captain Smith then handed over the "Master's Report to Company" to White Star's marine superintendent, Benjamin Steele. It read, "I herewith report this ship loaded and ready for sea. The engines and boilers are in good order for the voyage, and all charts and sailing directions up-to-date. Your obedient servant, Edward J. Smith."

The first passengers began to arrive at 9:30AM when the boat train carrying second- and third-class passengers completed its two-hour journey from London's Waterloo station. Of the 497 third-class passengers leaving from Southampton, 180 (including 30 children) were Scandinavian, as a result of White Star's extensive advertising campaign in Norway and Sweden. The majority were heading for a new life in the United States and had booked their passage aboard "the first available ship." It was to be their misfortune that the first available ship was the *Titanic*.

Notable among the 183 British third-class passengers embarking at Southampton were two large families — the Sages and the Goodwins. John and Annie Sage boarded with their nine children and Fred and Augusta Goodwin had six, the youngest being baby Sidney. Having sold their house in London, the Goodwins were emigrating to America, where electrical engineer Fred was preparing to join his brother Thomas in work at a new power station. They had been booked to travel on a smaller steamer, but their passage had been canceled because of the coal strike. Instead the booking was transferred to the glamorous *Titanic*, where third-class would be as good as first-class on that other ship. The Goodwins, like the Sages, were tremendously excited. Yet not one member of these two large families would make it to New York.

The second- and third-class entrances were both on C deck, although naturally they were separate. In their rooms, passengers found maps to guide them around the maze of corridors. Among the 245 people in second-class was seven-year-old Eva Hart, who was traveling to Winnipeg with her father Benjamin and mother Esther. Benjamin Hart, an Essex builder,

A sense of tremendous expectation hung in the cool spring air.

☆

THE HART FAMILY
They were en route to a new life in Canada. Seven-year-old Eva survived.

had decided to start a new life in Canada. The Harts too had been due to sail on another ship — the *Philadelphia* — only for their plans to be scuppered by the coal strike. But Mrs Hart was far from enthusiastic about the impending voyage. She was particularly concerned about the "unsinkable" label that had been bestowed upon the *Titanic*, considering such a declaration to be tantamount to blasphemy. "That is flying in the face of God," she told her husband. "That ship will never get to the other side of the Atlantic." Even as they boarded the ship, Mrs. Hart pleaded with her husband to turn back, but he refused and reluctantly she joined him and Eva in their cabin. Once there, she refused to venture out, except for meals. Convinced that disaster would overtake the ship at night, she chose to sleep during the daytime and to stay awake during the hours of darkness. Little Eva Hart was to owe her life to her mother's night-time vigil.

Many of the 202 first-class passengers embarking at Southampton arrived on the 11:30AM boat train, which had left Waterloo at 9:45AM, and were shown to their sumptuous cabins. As noon drew nearer, pilot George Bowyer, who had been in charge of the *Olympic* when she was struck by H.M.S. *Hawke*, prepared for departure. On the stroke of noon, with crowds lining the quayside waving farewell to their loved ones, three loud blasts on the *Titanic*'s mighty whistles announced that she was in motion. As she was cast off, eight crew

members, including the three Slade brothers, who had left the ship for a last-minute pint at a nearby pub, raced along the pier in a desperate attempt to scramble aboard. Two just reached the gangway before it was raised — the other six were left behind on the dock, cursing their luck.

A near miss

Pulled by six tugs because she was not yet under her own power, the *Titanic* crept out of the slip and into the channel of the River Test. There she was carefully maneuvered to port and released by the restraining tugs. Free at last and under her own power, she began to pick up speed, reaching around six knots. Negotiating the narrow channel constituted a delicate piece of navigation for any sizable ship, but with a liner as vast as the *Titanic*, it was fraught with potential problems. The space was further restricted by the presence of two liners, *Oceanic* and *New York*, tied up in tandem (with the latter on the outside) at berths 38 and 39. Normally, only one ship would have been tethered there, but more vessels than usual were docked at Southampton that day, waiting for clearance to sail after the coal strike.

After passing the two smaller liners, the *Titanic* was to make another turn to port into the River Itchen before heading out to sea. But first there was high drama, caused by the same problem that had resulted in the collision between the *Olympic* and H.M.S. *Hawke*. As the *Titanic* approached the 517-foot-long *New York*, the turbulence caused by her forward movement washed innocuously into the River Test on her starboard side. But on her port side, where the *New York* was berthed, the displaced water had nowhere to go. With the *Titanic* now alongside, the surge of water from her swept the *New York* up and down with such force that the *New York*'s six mooring lines snapped. A series of sharp cracks, like pistol shots, rang out across the Test. The *Titanic* forged ahead, leaving in her wake further waves, which had the effect of drawing the unshackled *New York* inexorably towards her. As the stern of the *New York* swung to within three or

four feet of the *Titanic*'s port side, a collision appeared inevitable.

"Full astern"

The day was saved by Captain Gale of the *Vulcan*, one of the tugs escorting the *Titanic*. Alert to the danger, but not wishing to end up as the meat in a sandwich between the two liners, he managed to swing his tug behind the *New York*'s stern and, at the second attempt, to get a line over her. This succeeded in slowing her drift towards the *Titanic*. At the same time, on the bridge of the *Titanic*,

Captain Smith and Pilot Bowyer reacted quickly to the danger. Bowyer ordered "Stop engines" then "Full astern" and Smith had the starboard anchor lowered to just above the level of the water, ready for dropping in the event of a sudden turn. By these combined efforts, contact between the two liners was averted and the *Titanic* reversed slowly back towards White Star Dock. Further tugs raced to the aid of the *Vulcan* and succeeded in finally bringing the *New York* under control. It had been a very close call.

Captain Gale gave his version of events to the

A SIZE THAT WAS HARD TO HANDLE
Maneuvering Titanic *and her sister ships proved to be a delicate and accident-prone operation.*

THE CAFE PARISIEN
This soon became the haunt of younger passengers.

Southampton Times and Hampshire Express, describing how he had first helped the *Titanic* out of her new dock. "We let go by the starboard quarter and dropped astern in order to go alongside and pick up a number of workmen who were about to leave the *Titanic*. The *Titanic* was drawing about 35 feet of water and she was near the sea bed. As soon as she drew abreast of the *New York* her ropes snapped, caused either by the backwash or suction, and I turned the *Vulcan* round and got a wire rope on the port quarter of the *New York*, and got her clear of the *Titanic*."

While acknowledging that the incident had "caused considerable consternation among the hundreds of people on the quayside," the paper was quick to rush to the defense of Captain Smith, endeavoring to quash any accusations that he may have been traveling too fast. It wrote of the *Titanic*'s departure: "From the moment she began to move from her berth she was under absolute control, and she passed out of the dock not only majestically, but also smoothly and calmly. If anything, she was proceeding more slowly than the *Olympic* usually does."

deck of the *Titanic* may have laughed off the incident with the *New York* as a trivial affair, with no damage done, but those who already harbored misgivings about the great liner were surely convinced that they were now aboard an unlucky, even doomed, ship.

First port of call

The second departure from Southampton was uneventful and, after Pilot Bowyer had been dropped off, the *Titanic* was soon out in the English Channel, bound for her first port of call, Cherbourg in Normandy. It was a journey of under 80 miles, but it took just over four hours.

Cherbourg had been a regular port of call for White Star liners since 1907, when the company began its Southampton–New York service. However, it was a relatively small port and, unlike Southampton and New York, where specially enlarged piers and docks had been created to cater for the *Titanic* and her sister ship, Cherbourg could not accommodate the largest of liners. So the *Titanic* had to drop anchor outside the harbor while passengers and cargo were ferried out by two purpose-built White Star tenders, *Nomadic* and *Traffic*.

The *Titanic* arrived in Cherbourg at 6:35PM, local time, having made no attempt to make up the hour lost at Southampton. Twenty-two passengers (15 first-class and seven second-class) had been using the *Titanic* as nothing more than a cross-Channel ferry and duly alighted at this, their port of destination. Their crossing had cost them £1 10s for first-class and £1 second-class. Also taken off was a canary, belonging to a Mr. Meanwell. The human freight was replaced by 142 first-class passengers, 30 second-class and 102 third-class, all of whom had made the six-hour rail trip from the Gare St Lazare in Paris aboard the Train Transatlantique.

As at Southampton, the first-class passenger list was small but select. Foremost among them was the 47-year-old American mining king Benjamin Guggenheim. The family, descended from Swiss emigrants, had made their fortune in smelting in the appropriately named Leadville, Colorado, although Guggenheim also owned a mining plant in Britain.

Smith and Bowyer may have performed with more alacrity than they did on board the *Olympic*, but it would appear that they had learned little from the previous escapade and were still traveling too quickly for such a confined area. The near miss delayed *Titanic*'s departure for another hour, to allow additional lines to be attached to the *Oceanic*, the liner with which the *New York* was moored in tandem, so there was no repeat performance when *Titanic* steamed past again. Whatever else, it was an ominously bad start to a new ship's career at sea. Many of those who had looked on helplessly from the

BENJAMIN GUGGENHEIM

His chauffeur traveled separately on a second-class ticket.

LUCY, LADY DUFF GORDON

The international fashion designer, her husband Sir Cosmo Duff Gordon and her secretary survived. Sir Cosmo's conduct during the evacuation was later investigated by the British Court of Inquiry into the Titanic disaster.

He was reported to be worth $58 million, but this proved to be something of an exaggeration. Guggenheim was joined on board the *Titanic* by his valet, Victor Giglio, and his chauffeur, René Pernot, the latter opting to travel separately on a second-class ticket.

There were a number of other rich Americans, including the Cardezas (who, as the saying goes, had enough luggage to sink a ship), businessman Emil Brandeis and Denver millionairess Mrs. James Joseph Brown, known to her friends as "Molly." She had met the Astors while on holiday in Egypt and was keen to return to the United States on the same crossing as them. Luckily for her — and, as it turned out, a number of survivors — this redoubtable lady was able to switch her original reservation to the *Titanic*.

The first-class boarders also included a middle-aged English couple traveling under the name of "Mr. and Mrs. Morgan," although in reality they were international dress designer Lucy, Lady Duff Gordon (who traded under the name of "Lucile" from premises in London's fashionable Hanover Square) and her Eton-educated husband, Sir Cosmo Duff Gordon. Quite why the couple should choose to travel incognito, in separate cabins, remains a mystery, as does their choice of "Morgan" as an alias. Was it perhaps an in-joke at the expense of J. Pierpont Morgan?

The third-class passengers who joined the ship at Cherbourg were of Middle Eastern extraction and with little command of English. After one and a half hours at the French port, the *Titanic* was ready to depart. Three deep booms on her whistles and she headed off into the night, bound for Queenstown, her last stop before the wide open seas of the Atlantic.

Final port of call

Like Cherbourg, Queenstown was too small to accommodate a liner the size of the *Titanic* and so, when she arrived at 11:30AM on the 11th, anchor was dropped two miles off shore. Two White Star tenders, *America* and *Ireland*, then ferried the 113 third-class and seven second-class passengers, plus 1,385 sacks of mail, out to the waiting *Titanic*. As usual, even on these tenders, the passengers were segregated by class.

Seven passengers, who had each paid £4 to travel first-class from Southampton, disembarked. Among them was 32-year-old teacher and student priest Francis Browne. A keen photographer, Browne took the last surviving pictures from aboard the *Titanic*, including a poignant shot of Captain Smith gazing down from the bridge.

In the frenzied activity that accompanies any stopover, one crewman managed to desert ship. John

THE TURKISH BATHS
Through a carved Cairo curtain, "the light fitfully reveals something of the grandeur of the mysterious East."

Coffey, a 24-year-old fireman born in Queenstown, hid in a pile of mailbags and smuggled himself ashore. It would appear that he had used the *Titanic* as a means of getting a free trip home.

During the wait at Queenstown, passengers on the *Titanic* were able to buy goods from a flotilla of small boats that had sailed out with the White Star tenders. From one of these enterprising salesmen, Colonel John Jacob Astor bought a £165 lace shawl for his young wife. But there was a jarring note when those on board spotted a blackened, soot-covered face at the top of the aftermost of the *Titanic*'s four funnels. This was in fact a dummy funnel, employed as a ventilator rather than a chimney, and one of the stokers had decided to climb the ladder inside for a prank. Some laughed at the sight, but others saw it as another portent of doom.

At 1:30PM, the *Titanic*, now with the American flag flying, left Queenstown to begin the long haul across the Atlantic to New York, where she was due to arrive on the morning of April 17. As the ship's engines thundered into action, passenger Eugene Daly, newly boarded at Queenstown, played a mournful tune on the bagpipes called "Erin's Lament." It was a form of farewell to his beloved country. Soon the green hills of Ireland receded into the distance and the *Titanic* vanished over the horizon. Three-quarters of those on board would never see land again.

CHAPTER THREE
AND THE BAND
PLAYED ON

The frozen land mass of Greenland produces an average of 12,000 to 15,000 icebergs every year. Around 400 drift far enough south to endanger transatlantic shipping. But numbers are irrelevant. As the *Titanic* found to her cost, one iceberg can be sufficient to sink the biggest liner in the world.

NO RESCUE *As the first distress rocket was fired, several of the* **Titanic's** *officers saw the masthead lights of another ship.*

As the *Titanic* steamed west along the ordained North Atlantic route, not even the most apprehensive of her passengers could have foreseen a problem with ice. The sky was blue, the winds light, and the ocean calm — perfect sailing weather. Indeed the winter of 1912 had been the mildest in those parts for more than 30 years. Yet it was that mildness that caused huge ice fields to break away from the mass and drift south, where the winter had been severe enough to ensure there was no warm air to melt them. During the week beginning April 7, as many as 20 ships reported seeing ice in the area. Some were forced to stop by immense icebergs and one — the French Line's *Niagara* — sustained minor damage. These ships' observations indicated a vast ice field stretching from 46°N to 41°31'N and from 46°18'W to 50°40'W. The *Titanic*'s course would take her to 42°N, 47°W — right into the middle of the ice.

Oblivious to the deadly obstacles that lay in her path, the *Titanic* pressed on, forever westward. Between noon on Friday the 12th and Saturday the 13th, she covered 519 miles; and from Saturday to Sunday, a further 546 miles. The ship was building up steam and 24 of her 29 boilers were in use. Weather permitting, J. Bruce Ismay had planned a brief speed trial for Monday 15th when, for the first time, the *Titanic* might travel flat out at around 24 knots. Contrary to rumors among some passengers, there was to be no attempt at a record crossing — the *Mauretania*'s 26-knot performance put such a target well out of reach.

On board, the passengers relaxed in the sumptuous surroundings; the clear starlit nights made the trip all the more memorable, especially for the newlyweds enjoying their honeymoon. But there was little peace for the ship's Marconi wireless operators, 24-year-old Jack Phillips and 22-year-old Harold Bride, who were kept fully employed by first-class passengers who were eager to impress their friends by sending messages home from the *Titanic*. The apparatus was particularly popular at night, when its transmitting range trebled to around 1,200 miles. Although the service was not cheap — a

1912

APRIL 11

1:30 PM

Titanic *departs Queenstown in Ireland.*

minimum fee of 12s 6d (or $3) for 10 words, and 9d per word thereafter — money was no object to those in the finest staterooms.

First warnings of ice

Sunday, April 14, 1912, dawned like any other day. One of the first passengers to rise was Colonel Archibald Gracie, who wasted no time in engaging Frederick Wright, the ship's squash professional, in a pre-breakfast warm-up. Still with energy to burn, the Colonel went for a dip in the swimming pool before emerging to eat a hearty breakfast. The crew went about their business as usual — with a certain amount of relief in some quarters, since the troublesome fire in number six boiler-room had finally been extinguished the previous evening. Sunday was the one day in the week when Captain Smith was not required to make a detailed tour of inspection, but any thoughts of a quiet morning were ruined as early as 9:00AM when the ship received a two-day-old wireless message from Captain Barr of the Cunarder *Caronia*, which was journeying east from New York to Liverpool. It read:

"Captain, *Titanic* — Westbound steamers report bergs, growlers and field ice in 42 degrees North from 49 degrees to 51 degrees West, April 12. Compliments, Barr."

Growler is a nautical term for a small iceberg. After reading the message, which was delivered to him on the bridge, Captain Smith had it posted for his officers and then at 10:30AM he led a religious service in the first-class dining saloon. All present joined in the "Prayer for those at Sea." In second class, the service was conducted by the purser.

The area referred to in the wireless message lay just a few miles north of the *Titanic*'s intended course and all the while there was the southerly drift of ice to take into consideration. At 11:40AM, the

"Captain, Titanic *– Westbound steamers report bergs, growlers and field ice ..."*

☆

1912

APRIL 13

1:00PM

Chief engineer reports that a fire in coal-bunker number 10 is extinguished.

Dutch liner *Noordam* also reported ice in much the same position.

Sunday morning on White Star ships was supposed to include a boat drill where all hands, passengers and crew, would assemble in life jackets at their boat stations. Yet on this occasion, Captain Smith omitted to call a drill. Perhaps he deemed the *Titanic* to be so secure that the exercise was unnecessary, or maybe he feared that the shortage of lifeboats would unduly alarm any nervous passengers.

At 1:42PM, the *Titanic* received another ice warning, this time from the *Baltic*. The message read: "Captain Smith, *Titanic* — Greek steamer *Athinai* reports passing icebergs and large quantities of field ice today in latitude 41°51'N, longitude 49°52'W." At the time, the *Titanic* was at 42°35'N, 45°50'W. The ice was perilously close to the ship's course.

The message was taken instantly to the bridge, but instead of showing it to his officers, Captain Smith took it with him when he went down for lunch. On the promenade deck, he bumped into J. Bruce Ismay and handed him the message for information. Ismay promptly put it in his pocket. Apart from Ismay showing it to a few select passengers, the piece of paper stayed there for the next five-and-a-half hours, until the master asked for its return and had it posted on the bridge. Given that passenger safety was supposed to be paramount, the behavior of both men is baffling, to the point of negligence. One can only assume that they underestimated the threat. But Smith was a very experienced seaman and should have realized that even a ship the size of the *Titanic* could not afford to take chances with icebergs.

The ice was closing in. Silently, imperceptibly, the immense icebergs floated across the ocean like a mobile mountain range. At 1:45PM, three minutes after the message from the *Baltic*, the German liner *Amerika* reported to the U.S. Navy's Hydrographic Office in Washington that she had passed two large icebergs at 41°27'N, 50°8'W. The Hydrographic Office relayed the information to North Atlantic shipping and it was picked up by Jack Phillips on the *Titanic*. According to his junior, Harold Bride, Phillips kept the warning to himself and failed to notify an officer.

A cold, clear night

That afternoon, the temperature dropped sharply. Passengers abandoned the decks in favor of the warm public rooms. Colonel Gracie finished reading a book and returned it to the library. Others in first-class settled in the smoking room or the reading room, or took afternoon tea before a blazing fire in the lounge, while listening to a trio from the ship's orchestra playing a selection of popular music — from Gilbert and Sullivan or Strauss to ragtime, the latest craze. The second- and third-class public rooms were equally busy, but their occupants had to provide their own entertainment. Elsewhere, bright-eyed children wandered the endless corridors, still coming to terms with the awesome splendor of the *Titanic*.

At 5:50PM, the *Titanic* reached the "Corner", at 42°N, 47°W, and changed her course from S62°W to S86°W. Down below, passengers were preparing for dinner in their respective dining saloons. The sounding of the bugle was the signal for a legion of stewards, stewardesses, maids, and valets to spring into action and assist first-class passengers in their sartorial preparations. As usual, the big social event of the evening was to take place in the à la carte restaurant, where the Wideners were hosting a party for Captain Smith. Other guests included the Thayers, the Carters, and Archie Butt. On his way down to the restaurant Captain Smith again encountered J. Bruce Ismay and finally acquired the earlier ice warning from the *Baltic*.

As darkness descended, navigation became more important than ever. An iceberg watch was ordered,

1912	9:00 AM	1:42 PM	1:45 PM
APRIL 14	*Caronia reports ice at latitude 42°N, extending from longitude 49° to 50°W.*	*Titanic's position 42° 35'N, 45°50'W. Baltic reports ice 41° 50'N, 49°52'W.*	*Amerika reports ice 41°27'W, 50°8'W.*

although the necessary vigilance was not helped by the lack of a pair of binoculars in the crow's nest. A pair had been at hand when the *Titanic* had left Belfast, but by the time the ship departed from Southampton eight days later, they had vanished. According to the subsequent testimony of Second Officer Charles Herbert Lightoller, there were no fewer than five pairs scattered around the bridge —

but none where they were needed most. Only one-ninth of an iceberg is visible above the surface of the water and sometimes after a berg has capsized, the water in the upper area can make its new face dark, or blue, which makes early identification at night extremely difficult, especially without binoculars. First Officer William Murdoch, an experienced sailor, was anxious that nothing should impair vision

THE WIDENERS
Their party in honor of Captain Smith was to be the final entry in a number of first-class passengers' social diaries.

1912	5:50 PM	7:00 PM	7:15 PM
APRIL 14	Titanic *turns the corner at* 42°N, 47°W, *changing course from S62°W to S86°W.*	Air temperature 43°F.	Ice warning from Baltic *finally posted on bridge.*

from the crow's nest or the bridge. So at 7:15PM, while making his rounds, he ordered the forward forecastle hatch to be closed, fearing that the light from it might interfere with the lookouts. He told lamp trimmer Samuel Hemming, "When you go forward, see the fore scuttle is closed as we are in the vicinity of ice ... and I want everything dark before the bridge."

Beneath the starlit sky, it was getting colder by the minute. By 7:30PM, the temperature had dropped to 39°F. At that moment, the *Titanic*'s wireless room intercepted a message from the Leyland freighter *Californian* to the eastbound *Antillian*. It reported three large icebergs at 42°3'N, 49°9'W, some 19 miles north of the *Titanic*'s course. Harold Bride said he took the message to the bridge and handed it to an officer, although he was later unable to remember which one. Meanwhile, Captain Smith was still being entertained by the Wideners.

Within an hour and a half, the temperature had dipped to 33°F, barely above freezing point. Second Officer Lightoller, who had relieved Murdoch as officer of the watch, warned ship's carpenter Maxwell, who was responsible for the freshwater tanks, that the water in them might freeze. When Captain Smith arrived on the bridge shortly before 9:00PM, Lightoller, 38, who had been at sea since the age of 13, briefed him on the prevailing conditions. Although Smith had deliberately left the party early because the *Titanic* was expected to encounter ice before midnight, neither man appeared unduly concerned, especially as visibility was good. They discussed the flat calm of the ocean and Lightoller remarked that it was a pity the earlier breeze had subsided because icebergs were easier to spot at night if the wind stirred up some surf. But they agreed that even if the berg "showed a blue side," they would have sufficient warning. With that, at

around 9:30PM, Smith retired to his cabin after telling Lightoller to keep him informed of any deterioration in visibility or weather conditions.

The unheeded message

Harold Bride had also decided to take a break before preparing himself for the rush of late-night messages, so the wireless apparatus was manned solely by Jack Phillips. At 9:40PM, Phillips took a message from the westbound S.S. *Mesaba*: "From *Mesaba* to *Titanic* and all eastbound ships. Ice report in latitude 42°N to 41°25'N, longitude 49°W to 50°30'W. Saw much heavy pack ice and great number large icebergs. Also field ice. Weather good, clear."

Because the land station at Cape Race in Newfoundland was now within range, Phillips was apparently preoccupied with transmitting messages that had accumulated during the day. Consequently, the message from the *Mesaba* was put to one side and never delivered to Captain Smith or the bridge. It was a fatal oversight, for the warning pinpointed the precise spot where the *Titanic* was to meet her doom.

Yet even if the message had reached those in authority, there is little to suggest they would have acted upon it. The *Mesaba*'s was the sixth ice warning received by the *Titanic* that day. If the locations given had been properly charted, it would have immediately become apparent that the *Titanic* was heading straight for a vast belt of ice, stretching some 78 miles across her path. Instead it seems that most of the warnings were casually dismissed on the bridge, where an air of complacency reigned. Certainly, no consideration seems to have been given to reducing the *Titanic*'s speed of 22½ knots, unless the visibility grew noticeably worse. Captain Smith was convinced that, on such a brilliantly clear night, any iceberg could be spotted in ample time.

1912	7:30 PM	8:40 PM	9:00 PM
APRIL 14	Californian *reports ice* 42°3'N, 49°9'W.	*Second Officer Lightoller warns crow's nest to watch for ice and orders ship's carpenter Maxwell to watch the fresh water supply in case it freezes.*	*Air temperature 33°F.*

ICEBERG
From 50 to 100 feet according to various accounts

← Starboard port holes

A GLANCING BLOW
First Officer Murdoch gave orders which prevented a head-on collision. The massive liner nevertheless ground up against a towering mountain of ice.

9:40 PM

*Mesaba reports ice
42°N to 41°25'N, 49°W to 50°30'W.
Warning not passed on to bridge.*

There was nothing unusual in Smith's behavior. The majority of captains, faced with increasingly tight schedules, preferred to forge ahead in the face of possible adversity. Those who erred on the side of caution were treated with disdain. Captain James Barr of the *Caronia* was nicknamed "Foggy" because of his tendency to reduce speed at the first hint of haze.

At 10:00PM, First Officer Murdoch took over on the bridge from Lightoller and remarked on the cold. The air temperature had dropped to freezing and the water temperature was now down to 31°F. For the previous half-hour, on Lightoller's orders, lookouts Archie Jewell and George Symons had been keeping their eyes open for ice. So when Reginald Lee and Frederick Fleet replaced them in the cramped crow's nest, 50 feet up the forward mast above the forecastle deck, the message was passed on. Before handing over to Murdoch, Lightoller commented, "We might be up around the ice any time now." With that, he finished his rounds and turned in.

At the heart of the *Titanic*, things were beginning to wind down for the night. There was no dancing aboard White Star ships on Sundays and many of the passengers had retired to their cabins by 11:00PM. Exhausted by his hectic day and with the prospect of another early start tomorrow, Colonel Gracie had made his excuses and left the first-class dining saloon at 9:30PM. The first-class reception room was almost deserted now that the band had finished for the evening, and there was scarcely more activity in the Café Parisien, except for a party hosted by Archie Butt. Those men in first-class who yearned for the nightlife made their way to the smoking room where the tables were arranged for bridge. Others preferred to slump back in the big leather chairs and read. On a night such as this, they were just grateful for the warmth.

In the wireless room, Jack Phillips was busy

dealing with the Cape Race traffic when, at 11:00PM, he was suddenly interrupted by a loud signal from the nearby *Californian*, announcing, "We are stopped and surrounded by ice." Angry at the intrusion, which must have almost deafened him, Phillips retorted, "Shut up, shut up. You're jamming my signal. I'm busy. I'm working Cape Race." Before the *Californian* could give her position, some 20 miles north of the *Titanic*, she was unceremoniously cut off. The *Californian*'s wireless operator, Cyril Furmstone Evans, listened patiently for another quarter of an hour or so before giving up.

A menacing black shape

With six expert lookouts, the *Titanic* carried more than any other ship afloat. They worked in pairs, two hours on and four hours off. In the crow's nest, there was little conversation between Lee and Fleet as they scoured the ocean for signs of danger, while desperately trying to keep out the cold. With only 30 minutes left on watch, they were eagerly anticipating the warmth of their bunks. Besides, it required all their concentration to pick out any hazards ahead. Shortly after 11:30PM, Lee and Fleet became aware of a misty haze on the horizon. A few minutes later, at 11:40PM, Fleet peered out once more into the darkness and saw all his worst nightmares in one menacing black shape. Without a word to his colleague, he rang the 16-inch brass bell in the crow's nest three times and lifted the telephone to the bridge.

Sixth Officer James Moody answered. Fleet's message was chillingly brief: "Iceberg right ahead."

"Thank you," replied Moody.

Out of the darkness, Fleet could see the pinnacled shape of the iceberg moving nearer by the second to the starboard bow of the *Titanic*. Witnesses described it as being of a similar shape to the Rock of Gibraltar. On the bridge, William Murdoch responded to the message from the crow's nest by giving the order, "Hard a-starboard." Under the system of helm orders then in force, this meant the ship's bow would swing to port. At the same time, he gave an order to the engine room, "Stop.

1912	10:00PM	10:30PM	11:00PM
APRIL 14	*Air temperature 32°F. Lookouts Lee and Fleet begin watch in the crow's nest.*	*Sea temperature plunges to 31°F.*	*Californian tries to warn of ice, but is cut off before she can give location.*

Full speed astern." Acting swiftly, he also pushed a bell-button for 10 seconds to warn those below that he intended to close all the ship's much-vaunted watertight doors. He then pulled the switch that automatically closed them.

But it was too late. Subsequent evidence suggested that Fleet had spotted the iceberg at a distance of less than 500 yards. At her trials, the *Titanic* had taken 850 yards to stop when traveling at 20 knots. Here, approaching an ice field, she was doing 22½, covering 38 feet per second. There was no way she could stop in time. Murdoch's actions

"A SLIGHT SHOCK, A SLIGHT TREMBLING"
The huge impetus of the **Titanic** *traveling at 22½ knots carved large chunks of ice from the iceberg, some of which fell onto the forward well deck.*

APRIL 14

11:40 PM

Titanic *collides with iceberg.*

A NARROW GASH

The size of the gouge in the **Titanic's** *hull was only 12 square feet, but this was damage above the ship's much-vaunted double bottom.*

avoided a head-on collision and, briefly, as the ship's bow started to veer away from the approaching berg, looked capable of averting contact altogether. But there was no time to turn more than two points to port. All he succeeded in doing was changing the impact to a glancing blow, which, as it transpired, was the worst possible scenario. Just 40 seconds after Frederick Fleet's warning, an ominous scraping sound signaled the beginning of the end for the *Titanic*.

The ice mountain was at least 75 feet above water level as it slid by on the starboard side, dwarfing those on board the liner. As it moved along the side of the ship, it scraped along the first 300 feet of the hull, way below the waterline. Large chunks of ice fell on to the forward well deck. As the berg passed amidships, Murdoch ordered the helm hard to port in order that the stern would clear. The berg passed beyond the stern and drifted silently away into the distance.

"Ripping and cutting noises"

Many passengers were totally unaware that there had been a collision and a number even managed to sleep through it. James Johnson, a steward in the first-class dining saloon, said, "I did not feel much because we thought she had lost her wheel or something, and somebody passed the remark, 'another Belfast trip' (for an unscheduled repair)."

Lady Duff Gordon was preparing for bed in cabin A20 at the moment of impact. She described it as though "someone had drawn a giant finger all along the side of the boat." Another first-class passenger, Mrs. J. Stuart White in cabin C32, was equally colorful and dismissive about the incident: "It did not seem to me there was any great impact at all. It was

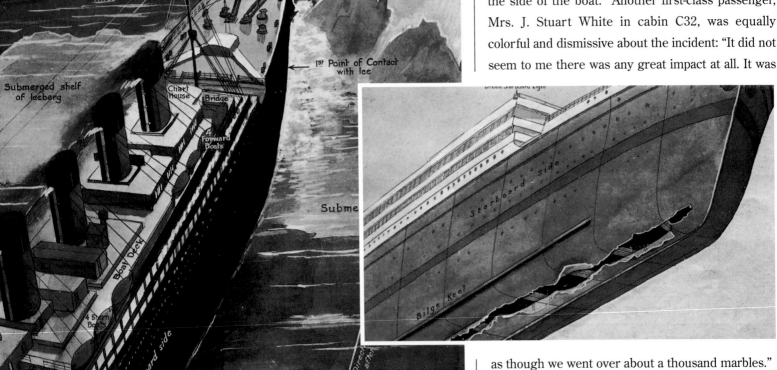

Marconi Wires

1st Point of Contact with Ice

Submerged shelf of Iceberg

Chart House

Bridge

4 Forward Boats

Boat Deck

4 Stern Boats

Starboard side

Starboard side

Direction after

Submerged Bulk of Iceberg

Green Starboard Light

Starboard side

Bilge Keel

Subme

as though we went over about a thousand marbles."

In second-class cabin D56, young teacher Lawrence Beesley was wakened, but felt "nothing more than what seemed to be an extra heave of the engines and a more than usually obvious dancing of the mattress on which I sat. Nothing more than that

— no sound of a crash or of anything else; no sense of shock, no jar that felt like one heavy body meeting another."

J. Bruce Ismay was also roused by the collision, but attributed it to the belief that the ship had lost a blade from the propeller.

Able Seaman Joseph Scarrott thought it was "just a trembling," while trimmer Thomas Dillon, who was on duty in the engine room, experienced only "a slight shock."

Others on board described a jarring or scraping sound. Martha Stephenson said she was asleep in first-class when she was "awakened by a terrible jar with ripping and cutting noises, which lasted for a few moments." Lookout George Symons added, "What awakened me was a grinding sound on her bottom. I thought at first she had lost her anchor and chain and it was running along her bottom." And Second Officer Lightoller recalled "a slight shock, a slight trembling and a grinding sound."

The water floods in

But it was a different story down in number six boiler room, on the starboard side of the ship, where leading fireman Frederick Barrett heard a sound like roaring thunder, followed by a flood of water cascading through a narrow gash in the ship's side some two feet above the stokehold floor. As the watertight doors closed, he was forced to escape up the boiler room's emergency ladder before the water engulfed him.

There was a more orderly evacuation of the first-class smoking room. The collision spilled one card player's drink and everyone jumped to their feet. The more inquisitive stepped out on to the promenade deck to investigate. There, someone remarked excitedly: "We hit an iceberg — there it is!"

Within a minute of the collision, Captain Smith had raced up to the bridge. "What have we struck?" he asked Murdoch.

"An iceberg, sir," came the reply. "I hard a-starboarded and reversed the engines and I was going to hard a-port around it, but she was too close. I could not do any more."

"Have you closed the watertight doors?"

"They are already closed, sir."

Fourth Officer Joseph Boxhall also hastened to the bridge. Smith instructed him to go below forward on the starboard side to ascertain the extent of the damage and to report back to him as quickly as possible. En route, Boxhall alerted the other officers, who hurried up to the bridge. Ismay had also arrived there to see what the commotion was about. As ordered, Boxhall reported back 15 minutes later, saying there was no sign of any damage above F deck, but that the orlop deck (the lowest) was flooded forward of number four watertight bulkhead and the five postal clerks who were working there in the mail room were shifting the sacks of mail to the post office on G deck above.

Their efforts would prove to be in vain. By midnight, when Captain Smith and Thomas Andrews of Harland & Wolff went below to inspect the damage for themselves, the mailbags were floating in feet of water. Andrews immediately recognized that the *Titanic* was a lost cause and gave her no more than two hours, possibly as little as one hour. The unsinkable ship was about to go down.

The iceberg, a rock-hard protrusion lurking invisibly beneath the ocean's surface, had sunk itself into the *Titanic*'s hull, then sliced along the steel plates, tearing a narrow 300-foot gash along her starboard side, above the double bottom. In the process, five of the supposedly watertight compartments were breached. The *Titanic* could float with any two compartments flooded, but five was too much for her to bear. Although only 12 square feet of the hull were gouged open by the collision, this was enough to sink her. The problem could be traced back to the transverse bulkheads. These upright partitions had not been extended high enough, so as the bow of the

"WHAT HAVE WE STRUCK?"
Captain Smith asked after racing to the bridge. He had retired for the night just over two hours before the collision.

APRIL 15	12:05 AM	12:10 AM	12:15 AM
	Captain Smith orders the lifeboats to be uncovered and the crew and passengers to be rounded up.	*Fourth Officer Boxhall estimates the* Titanic's *position to be 41°46'N, 50°14'W.*	Titanic *makes first wireless call for help. Lights from another ship spotted approximately six miles away.*

ship went down, adjoining compartments also filled up, like the sections in an ice-cube tray. As each compartment filled with water, the bow was pulled still further down, until the ship finally foundered.

Just 10 minutes after the collision, the water level had risen to 14 feet above the keel in the first five compartments. By five minutes past midnight, the floor of the squash court, 32 feet above the keel, was awash and water was

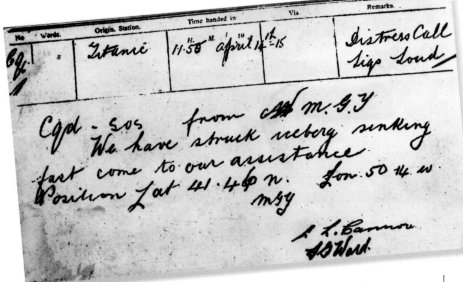

SOS
One of the ships to pick up the **Titanic's** *radioed distress call was the* **Birma.**

also pouring into boiler-room number five, the sixth watertight compartment. Already the great liner was beginning to sag at the head. Captain Smith knew there was not a minute to lose. At 12:05AM, he ordered the crew to be mustered and for them to stand by to uncover the lifeboats.

Meanwhile, in the dining saloons, stewards, unaware of the seriousness of the situation, prepared the tables for breakfast as usual.

Distress call

No sooner had he reported back on the damage than Fourth Officer Boxhall was asked by the master to calculate the ship's position. He came up with 41°46'N, 50°14'W, but it was a only a rough estimate. Boxhall wrote his answer on a piece of paper and Captain Smith took it to wireless operator Phillips, who was ordered to broadcast the international distress signal, CQD ("Come Quick, Danger") with the *Titanic's* position.

The first distress call was made at 12:15AM and was picked up by the French ship *La Provence*, the Canadian vessel *Mount Temple,* and the land station at Cape Race. However, the airwaves were crackling with messages that night and interference caused the position to be misinterpreted. By 12:25AM, the position was corrected under *Titanic's* call sign of MGY to the one Boxhall had calculated. "Come at once. We have struck a berg. It's a CQD. Position 41°46'N, 50°14'W."

Fifty-eight miles away, 21-year-old Harold Thomas Cottam was coming to the end of his day's work as the sole wireless operator on board the Mediterranean-bound Cunard liner *Carpathia*. In fact, Cottam had been on duty since 7:00AM the previous day. Not surprisingly, he was ready for bed and would have shut down his station half an hour earlier had he not been waiting for confirmation of receipt of a transmission he had sent to the liner *Parisian*. He had been passing the time listening to the land station at Cape Cod, which had a stack of messages for the *Titanic*. So when he located the *Titanic's* frequency and heard a rare moment of quiet, he asked whether Jack Phillips knew there was a pile of messages waiting for him. Almost before Cottam could finish, Phillips rushed out the distress message.

"Shall I tell my captain?" asked a flustered Cottam. "Do you require assistance?"

Phillips replied, "Yes. Come quick."

Cottam wasted no time in informing the bridge

and then Captain Arthur Henry Rostron, who had just gone to bed. Rostron's initial annoyance at Cottam bursting into his cabin turned to horror as he realized the full implications of the message. With speed and efficiency, he mobilized his men and soon the *Carpathia* was speeding to the rescue of the stricken *Titanic*.

Since there was no public address system on the *Titanic*, news filtered through to the passengers slowly, particularly because the vast majority were tucked up in their cabins. The first that some knew of the drama that was unfolding around them was when stewards knocked on their cabin doors and helped them on with lifebelts.

As the passengers began to assemble in the forward first-class entrance, they found themselves serenaded by Wallace Hartley and the ship's band who had regrouped there shortly after midnight. And when the passengers moved out on to the promenade and boat decks, ready for evacuation, the band duly transferred to a position outside the gymnasium. Their repertoire of relentlessly cheery ragtime tunes was meant to bolster spirits and reassure passengers that everything was under control and that there was no need for panic. Captain Smith, of course, knew otherwise — he was painfully aware that there were lifeboats for only 1,178 of the 2,207 people thought to be on board the *Titanic* that night.

Disorder and confusion

Smith ordered that women and children be loaded first. This was certainly the case on the port side, although on the starboard side, men were allowed to board if there were no women waiting. The ship's crew scarcely bathed themselves in glory as they loaded and lowered the boats. Their lack of training was all too apparent in some areas, particularly when operating the new Welin davits. Few crew members seemed to know the number of their boat station. Each crewman was assigned to a boat (they were required to row and steer the passengers to safety), but it seems that many had not bothered to read the lists that had been put up in the various quarters — or, if they had, they had forgotten the instructions.

The senior officers had originally intended that the boats should be lowered into the water half-full (they feared they were not strong enough to be lowered full to capacity) and then rowed to the big gangway doors in the side of the ship to take extra passengers. But the men sent down to open the doors were never seen again and the doors remained firmly closed. At around 12:45AM, Boxhall fired off the first distress rocket, an act he repeated at five-minute intervals. Briefly, it seemed that the *Titanic*'s prayers would be answered, for the lights of another ship were visible some six miles away to port. With the aid of binoculars, Boxhall had first noticed two masthead lights of a ship when he returned to the bridge after delivering the *Titanic*'s position to the Marconi room. Now, as he fired off the first rocket, he could see the ship approaching. Before long, his naked eye was able to make out her red port sidelight and green starboard lamp. Others on the bridge, including Captain Smith, also saw the lights. He ordered Boxhall and quartermaster George Rowe to attempt to contact the other ship via Morse lamp, as well as by firing rockets. But their desperate measures drew no response. An hour later,

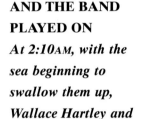

AND THE BAND PLAYED ON
At 2:10AM, with the sea beginning to swallow them up, Wallace Hartley and the **Titanic's** *musicians played one last tune.*

Over page
LAST MINUTE REPRIEVE
The lifeboats are lowered as the **Titanic** *begins to slip beneath the waves.*

"You'll have me drown the whole lot of them!"

☆

the mystery ship seemed to be turning away from the *Titanic* and it soon vanished into the night. With it went the hopes of most of those still on board the sinking ship.

While the first distress rocket was being fired, so the first lifeboat, number seven, was being lowered from the starboard side of the *Titanic* (odd numbered boats were on the starboard side, even numbers to port) on the orders of First Officer Murdoch. It had a capacity of 65, yet left less than half full, the maximum estimate of those aboard being 28. Among the first away were two of the lookouts, George Hogg and Archie Jewell, and first-class passenger Mrs. Helen Dickinson Bishop. Hogg, in particular, was praised by Mrs. Dickinson Bishop for his calm efficiency. At this stage, perhaps calmed by the band's jolly refrains, many passengers were reluctant to clamber into the lifeboats, wrongly concluding that they were perfectly safe on the ship. After all, the warmth of a brightly lit luxury liner must have seemed preferable to taking one's chances in a cold wooden boat, only to be tossed about on the dark seas of the North Atlantic.

In fact, boat number four should have been the first away, but the delay typified the lack of organization on board. It was the first boat ready and at around 12:30AM Captain Smith ordered Second Officer Lightoller to fill it from the promenade deck (A deck) instead of the boat deck as it would be less exposed for the women and children. Waiting to board on the boat deck above were some of the most influential first-class passengers — the Astors, the Wideners, the Carters, the Thayers and the Ryersons, all with their entourages. Hearing the change of plan, they duly trooped below, only for passenger Hugh Woolner to remind Captain Smith that the glass

windows on the promenade deck were closed. Smith, who had been confusing the ship with her sister, the *Olympic*, where the promenade deck was open, immediately ordered a return to the boat deck. By the time the passengers had climbed back up, the lifeboat had been lowered, as originally ordered, to the promenade deck. Lightoller then decided that it would be easier to have the windows opened than to haul the boat up again and so the passengers were again sent down to the promenade deck. With the women swathed in fur coats to protect them from the cold night air, they seem to have accepted such incompetence with remarkably good grace, although an exasperated Mrs. Thayer was heard to remark, "You ordered us up here and now you are taking us back!" It was another hour before boat number four was finally lowered into the sea.

Courage in a crisis

In the meantime, boat number five became the second to take to the water, at 12:55AM. Forty-one passengers, including several men, were shepherded in under the command of Third Officer Herbert Pitman. Wanting to appear useful, J. Bruce Ismay decided to intervene by hustling passengers aboard and then enthusiastically instructing Fifth Officer Harold Lowe to "lower away, lower away!" Lowe did not welcome the intrusion and firmly told his company chairman to get out of the way. "You want me to lower away quickly?" he demanded. "You'll have me drown the whole lot of them!" Suitably chastised, Ismay slunk off without a word.

Seeing his wife accept a seat in lifeboat number five and spotting the empty places beside her, Dr. Henry William Frauenthal decided that he and his brother Isaac should make a bold bid to join her. As the boat was lowered away, the brothers jumped

"LOWER AWAY, LOWER AWAY!"
The evacuation of the **Titanic** *was haphazard. At the start, lifeboats were launched half full, passengers either assuming they were safer on board or unaware of any emergency; the* **Titanic** *had no public-address system to warn them. At the end, there was panic and fighting for lifeboat places.*

from the deck into the moving craft. Unfortunately, the doctor landed on fellow first-class passenger, Mrs. Annie Stengel, breaking two of her ribs and knocking her unconscious in the process.

At about the same time as the departure of boat five, number six was lowered 70 feet into the sea from the port side. There were no more than 28 people aboard. They were all women, except for an Italian stowaway with a broken arm, plus two crew members — lookout Frederick Fleet, the man who had spotted the fatal iceberg, and quartermaster Robert Hichens. It was on this frail vessel that the legend of the "Unsinkable Molly Brown" was born. This Mrs. Brown was evidently a woman for a crisis, and crises did not come much bigger than this. She saw it as her job to rally the troops and stiffen resolve. Having ushered a few of her faint-hearted friends into the boat, she was about to set off to see where she could next be of most use when she was bundled into the descending lifeboat six by two acquaintances, Edward Calderhead and James McGough. After making the four-foot drop, she quickly ascertained that there were insufficient men aboard to row and

yelled out for the services of an experienced oarsman. Major Arthur Peuchen, a keen yachtsman, volunteered. The Major had left a box of securities worth £60,000 in his cabin, but had wisely decided that warm clothes were of more use than money.

Before the boat set off, Captain Smith ordered Hichens to row in the direction of the mystery ship, which at that time was still visible. But once in the water, Hichens steadfastly refused to row, leaving the

"THE UNSINKABLE MOLLY BROWN"
She was not the sort of woman to let a shipwreck daunt her spirits.

job to Fleet and Peuchen. (Other boats encountered difficulties with crewmen who could not row, simply because they had not been properly drilled in the skill. Additionally, some boats took to the water without the necessary equipment — a light, water, and biscuits. This was all part of the general inefficiency that was evident that night.)

Fleet and Peuchen tried manfully to propel the craft, but simply did not have the strength. So Molly Brown took off her life jacket, grabbed an oar and began rowing. Her efforts inspired some of the other women to lend a hand and together they guided the boat out to sea. Later, they met boat number 16 and took on board a stoker who was suffering badly from the cold. Mrs. Brown saved the man's life by wrapping her fur coat around him. She was a remarkable woman.

The next to load was boat three, with about 50 people on board, including 15 crew — far more than were needed to row. In the absence of sufficient women and children in the vicinity, Murdoch allowed men to board. Ten did so, but others — among them first-class passengers Charles M. Hays, Howard Case, Thornton Davidson and Washington Augustus Roebling II — gallantly assisted ladies into the boat before standing aside to help elsewhere. All four perished with the *Titanic*.

Fear and anger

The bow of the *Titanic* was now visibly sinking, to the extent that the water was lapping at her nameplate. It began to dawn on those still on board that the great ship was fighting a losing battle. A sense of orderly calm was replaced by one of anger, fear and confusion. Suddenly, there was no shortage of people wanting to fill the lifeboats, but officers remained reluctant to fill them to capacity in case the boats could not take the strain. Yet Harland & Wolff had conducted a test in which identical boats were lowered carrying the equivalent weight of 65 adults. Captain Smith and his colleagues appeared totally unaware of any such test.

The first of the two emergency cutters, boat number one, was launched at 1:10AM. It had a capacity of 40, yet was allowed to leave with just 12 people on board — seven crew and five passengers. In charge was lookout George Symons, who was instructed to lay off 200 yards and then return when summoned. The passengers included Sir Cosmo and Lady Duff Gordon and her secretary, Laura Francatelli. Sir Cosmo had been hanging around for some time in the hope of finding a boat in which the three of them might escape and so when an opportunity to board number one presented itself, he did not need asking twice. There has been much speculation about Sir Cosmo's lack of bravery on the night. After the *Titanic* had gone down and the icy seas were filled with people drowning or freezing to death, it was suggested that boat one should return to the scene to pick up survivors. But the idea appears to have been overruled and when it was revealed at the British inquiry into the tragedy that Sir Cosmo had offered each of the seven crewmen £5, this was interpreted as a bribe to ensure that they did not turn back and risk the boat being swamped and possibly capsized by taking on more people. The baronet, however, maintained the money was to replace their lost kit. Whatever the truth, the ensuing gossip left Sir Cosmo a broken man.

Boat number eight was also launched at 1:10AM and was the scene of one of the most touching moments of the whole drama. Isidor and Ida Straus watched as women were helped into the boat. When Mrs. Straus was asked to step in, she declined, saying, "I will not be separated from my husband. As we have lived, so we will die, together." When it was suggested that nobody could surely object to an elderly gentleman such as Mr. Straus occupying a place, he replied nobly, "No, I do not wish any distinction in my favor which is not granted to others." And so they stayed behind together to meet their fate after overseeing the safe departure of Mrs. Straus's maid, Ellen Bird, who tearfully accepted her mistress's fur stole as a farewell gift.

Thirty-nine made their escape aboard boat eight. The number included the redoubtable Countess of Rothes, who was given charge of the tiller and later helped with the rowing.

Molly Brown took off her life jacket, grabbed an oar and began rowing.

☆

1912	2:05 AM	2:17 AM	2:18 AM
APRIL 15	*Last lifeboat, collapsible D, lowered.*	*Last wireless signal sent.*	*Lights fail.*

Time begins to run out

At around 1:15AM, the *Titanic* suddenly lurched from starboard to port. She was becoming increasingly unstable, the deck tilting more and more steeply, making the process of evacuation even more difficult. All the while, the band played on. Quicksteps, marches, waltzes were all played with commendable fortitude, but by then, everyone realized the end was nigh.

Two more boats, nine and ten, were lowered at 1:20AM, their respective cargoes of 56 and 55 people indicating the heightened concern on board the sinking ship. The *Titanic*'s chief baker, Charles Joughin, helped throw young children across the daunting five-foot gap between the lifeboat and the side of the listing ship.

Boat 11 went off at 1:25AM with 70 aboard, closely followed by number 13 with 64, number 14 with 63, and number 15 with 70, mainly third-class women and children. The situation was now so desperate that officers were prepared to load the boats to their limits. The first signs of real panic were breaking out among those who were stranded and Fifth Officer Lowe was forced to brandish his gun to deter men from rushing the lifeboats. In the midst of the clamor for spaces, boat 12 was permitted to leave with just 42 on board, because of an apparent lack of women and children. When a group of men from second- and third-class tried to clamber aboard, the officers in charge held them at bay. According to one witness, a Frenchman leapt into the boat as it was being lowered past B deck. Wrestling with the ropes to lower the boats as quickly as possible, the crew induced a near calamity when boat 13 was almost crushed in the water beneath boat 15.

For those still on board the *Titanic*, time was running out fast ... and they knew it. Collapsible boat C was already two-thirds full when a group of

passengers tried to storm it. Chief purser Herbert McElroy responded by firing his pistol twice. As the men stepped back in alarm, none other than J. Bruce Ismay stealthily crept into the boat as it was lowered. Like Sir Cosmo Duff Gordon, Ismay was later pilloried for his behavior.

In the confusion, Lightoller seemed to have forgotten about boat number four, with its passenger list of wealthy women. It was finally launched at 1:55AM, after the eminent socialites had endured the ignominy of clambering out of the cranked-open windows on A deck. At first, 13-year-old John Ryerson was prevented from accompanying his mother, but the order was rescinded on the intervention of the boy's father. Colonel John Jacob Astor helped load the women and children, including his pregnant wife Madeleine. Since the boat was barely two-thirds full, Astor asked whether he might be allowed to join her, but Lightoller adhered firmly to the "women and children only" rule. Despite reassuring his wife that he would follow in another boat, Astor knew his chances of survival were negligible. As he waved a last good-bye to his young bride, he lit a cigarette and prepared to meet his fate. His last act was to dash down to the dog kennels on F deck where he managed to free his beloved Airedale, Kitty, as well as the other dogs. Madeleine Astor later said that her final memory of the *Titanic* was seeing Kitty running about on the sloping deck.

By 2:00AM, the water had risen to just 10 feet below the promenade deck, making the loading process more urgent than ever. The last lifeboat to be launched, collapsible D, went off at 2:05AM. Chief Officer Henry Wilde and Lightoller were in charge of loading. Lightoller drew his pistol and got crewmen to form a human barrier to hold back a sudden surge of men from steerage who had just arrived on the deck. It has been suggested in some quarters that

CHIEF OFFICER HENRY WILDE
With Second Officer Lightoller, he was in charge of launching the last lifeboat. Lightoller had to draw his pistol to restore order among the panicking passengers.

the reason for the last-minute appearance of hundreds of men and women from the third-class cabins was because barriers had been put in their way to prevent access to the upper decks, but there is no firm evidence to support this. Whatever caused their delay, by the time they reached the boat deck, it was too late. Within minutes, they were engulfed by the rising water and swept to their deaths.

Amid the crush of bodies on the boat deck, a second-class passenger calling himself Michel Hoffman managed to pass his two young sons, Michel and Edmond, through the human chain to a place of safety on the last boat. In fact, Hoffman's real name was Navratil, but he was traveling from Southampton under an assumed name, having snatched the children from their mother. As the boat was lowered past the open end of the promenade deck, Hugh Woolner and another first-class

2:20 AM	3:30 AM	4:10 AM
Titanic founders.	*Rockets from rescue ship* Carpathia *sighted by survivors in drifting lifeboats.*	*First lifeboat, number two, picked up by* Carpathia.

passenger, Mauritz Hakan Bjornstrom-Steffanson, seeing the water wash on to the deck and over their slippers, decided to make a jump for it. Luckily for them, they landed safely in the boat, which pulled away with 44 of its 47 places filled.

Valor and poignancy

As the end approached, acts of courage were taking place all over the ship. Chief steward Andrew Latimer gave his life jacket to a woman passenger before continuing to supervise the mass evacuation right up until the moment he went down with the ship. The 34 engineering officers stayed at their posts, maintaining the ship's lighting until two minutes before the ship finally sank. All were lost. Similarly, the five postal clerks, based in one of the first areas to be flooded, guarded the mailbags with their lives, until it was too late for them or their precious cargo to be rescued. It is thought that 3,364 bags of mail and some 800 parcels were lost that night.

There were poignant moments, too: chief baker Joughin slipping below for a swig of whisky from his private bottle and meeting one of the ship's surgeons on the same mission; Archie Butt, Arthur Ryerson, Frank Millet, and Clarence Moore finishing their game of cards in the first-class smoking room, before finally going up to the boat deck at 2:00AM; Benjamin Guggenheim and his valet, Victor Giglio, who went below and reappeared on deck in full evening dress with Guggenheim announcing, "We've dressed up in our best and are prepared to go down like gentlemen;" Harland & Wolff managing director Thomas Andrews sitting in the smoking room, staring blankly at the wall, frozen to the spot, his life jacket in front of him; and Colonel Gracie bumping into the squash professional, Frederick Wright, and wittily canceling his Monday morning half-hour on

FINAL MOMENTS
"The **Titanic's** *stern rose completely out of the water and went up 30, 40, 60 feet into the air. Then, with her body slanting at 45 degrees, slowly the* **Titanic** *slipped out of sight."*

the court, which was by then flooded to the ceiling.

And, of course, there was the band, playing on until all hope was lost. At around 2:10AM, with the sea about to swallow them, bandmaster Hartley informed his men that they had done their duty and could now save themselves if they so desired. To a man, all eight stood their ground and proceeded to play one last tune. With the noise made by the *Titanic*'s crumbling machinery as it lurched into the ocean and conflicting evidence from eyewitness accounts, nobody can be sure what that last tune was. Wireless operator Harold Bride reported hearing the hymn "Autumn" as he struggled for his life in the water, but this was

not on the official White Star music list. And it has been pointed out, not unreasonably, that playing in the dark on a steeply sloping deck, the band would have chosen a tune with which they were all familiar. Consequently, cases have been put forward for another hymn, "Nearer, My God, to Thee," and the popular waltz "Songe d'Automne," sometimes referred to as "Autumn."

The Titanic's last moments

At 2:17AM, her lights blazing defiantly and with more than 1,500 people still on board, the *Titanic* began to go under. As the bow plunged beneath the waves, washing many overboard, the last wireless call for help was sent out by Jack Phillips and Harold Bride, who had remained at their posts until the bitter end. With all about to be lost, Captain Smith told his men, "Do your best for the women and children, and look out for yourselves."

A minute later, the ship's lights flickered and went out. There was no moon that night and the only lights to guide survivors were the stars. As passengers and crew clung desperately to the deck rails, the stern of the *Titanic* rose into the air so that the great ship stood almost vertically for about 30 seconds. Inside, everything movable — all the luxurious furnishings and fittings, the tableware, the crockery — crashed along the hull with a deafening, thunderous roar. Then at 2:20AM, the stern flopped back into the water. Two of the four funnels broke off, releasing clouds of soot into the clear night sky. There was a series of explosions and the submerged forward section broke away from the stern. Finally, the stern also slipped beneath the surface and began its 2½-mile voyage to the bottom of the sea.

The *Titanic*'s end was witnessed from the water by Second Officer Lightoller, while he and around 30 other men clung for their lives to the upturned collapsible boat B. In the rush to launch all the lifeboats before the ship went down, there had been no time to release collapsibles A and B, which had been tethered to the roof of the officers' quarters

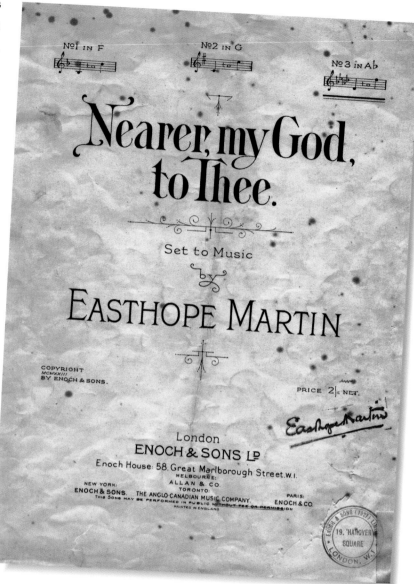

above the boat deck, and both were swept away as the sea swamped the decks. Officers Wilde and Murdoch were last seen trying to free boat B, but after it had fallen into the water upside down, neither man was able to scramble aboard. Two who did manage to reach the relative sanctuary of the upturned boat were Lightoller and Colonel Gracie. Both were dragged beneath the waves by the sinking ship, only to be blown suddenly back up to the surface by a surge of air forced through a ventilator. From there, they both managed to swim to the boat.

After being washed overboard, wireless operator Harold Bride was trapped in an air pocket beneath boat B for about 45 minutes. He finally succeeded in

THE LAST TUNE
The heroism of Wallace Hartley's band is part of Titanic *folklore, as is their last tune. But what was it? Eyewitness accounts differ.*

WENT DOWN WITH HIS SHIP?

Some reports suggest that Captain Smith reached collapsible boat B, then turned back. In any case his body was never found.

Previous page
HORRIFYING SIGHT
This artist's impression shows the lifeboats in the foreground as the **Titanic** *begins to sink.*

extricating himself and spent at least another half-hour in the sea before being picked up by boat 12. His ordeal in the freezing water had taken its toll. His ankles were gashed and bruised and his feet riddled with frostbite, but he survived. His colleague, Jack Phillips, was less fortunate. Abandoning ship at the very last minute, he somehow managed to reach boat B, but died of exposure in the middle of the night.

Fortified by whisky, baker Charles Joughin also spent what must have seemed like an eternity in the icy waters before locating boat B. At first he was pushed away, but eventually was allowed aboard as spaces were vacated by others in the boat toppling overboard to certain death through exhaustion and exposure.

The fate of Captain Smith remains a mystery as his body was never found. Some reports state that he was last seen with a child in his arms; others that he reached boat B and then decided to return to the sinking ship. But the most reliable witnesses say he stayed on the bridge until he went down with his ship.

Rescue arrives

According to the British Report into the disaster, as many as 50 people were saved by the last two collapsibles. First-class steward Edward Brown was one of the lucky ones who, after being washed off the boat deck, managed to struggle into boat A. He later recounted how people fought each other in the sea to get aboard. He himself had some of the clothes ripped from his back by dying men desperate to take his place. There was no room for dignity.

Boats A and B were eventually met by a flotilla of lifeboats assembled by Fifth Officer Harold Lowe, whose presence of mind saved a number of lives that night. Once afloat, he adopted the policy of safety in numbers by tying five of the boats together and rigging a mast and sail on number 14 to hasten the flotilla's progress towards the *Carpathia*. All the while, he was helping pick up survivors from the sea. By the time boat A was rescued, there was more than a foot of water inside. Those still alive were dragged on board Lowe's boat. The dead — and there were at least three — were left in the collapsible, which was then abandoned to drift away into the night.

The area close to where the *Titanic* went down was strewn with chairs and wooden debris, tossed into the sea at the last minute in the hope that they could be used as makeshift rafts. Further away, the lifeboats floated — some packed like sardines, others half empty. Beneath the starlit sky, heads could occasionally be seen bobbing up and down in the water. Faint cries for help could be heard. Soon the heads became fewer and the cries weaker, as exhausted bodies succumbed to the elements. The lucky ones on board the lifeboats had already cheated death once, but now, huddled together for warmth, would they be able to survive the night? Would they be rescued in time? Eyes regularly strained towards the horizon, praying for the sight of an approaching ship.

Fortunately for more than 700 of those fighting for their lives that night, the *Carpathia* was in good hands. No sooner had he received that first message from the stricken *Titanic* than Captain Rostron had organized his crew to provide maximum assistance. The ship's cabins and public rooms were prepared to receive the survivors, who would be given hot coffee and food. Portable lights and nets were draped along the side of the ship to facilitate boarding.

Eyewitness

Wearing only a bathrobe, Philadelphia banker Robert W. Daniel leapt from the sinking ship two minutes before she went down.

"Not until the last five minutes did the awful realization come that the end was at hand. The lights became dim and went out, but we could see. Slowly, ever so slowly, the surface of the water seemed to come up towards us. So gradual was it that even after I had adjusted the life jacket about my body it seemed a dream. Deck after deck was submerged. There was no lurching or grinding or crunching. The Titanic simply settled. I was far up on one of the top decks when I jumped. About me were many others in the water. My bathrobe floated away, and it was icily cold. I struck out at once. I turned my head, and my first glance took in the people swarming on the Titanic's deck. Hundreds were standing there helpless to ward off approaching death. I saw Captain Smith on the bridge. My eyes seemingly clung to him. The deck from which I had leapt was immersed. The water had risen slowly, and was now to the floor of the bridge. Then it was to Captain Smith's waist. I saw him no more. He died a hero. The bows of the ship were far beneath the surface, and to me only the four monster funnels and the two masts were now visible. It was all over in an instant. The Titanic's stern rose completely out of the water and went up 30, 40, 60 feet into the air. Then, with her body slanting at an angle of 45 degrees, slowly the Titanic slipped out of sight."

1912 APRIL 15	8:10 AM	8:30 AM	8:50 AM
	Final lifeboat, number 12, picked up.	*Californian comes alongside Carparthia.*	*Carparthia leaves for New York with survivors.*

The Carpathia's *passengers were the first outsiders to realize the full extent of the tragedy.*

☆

The *Carpathia* sped for the *Titanic's* last radioed position as fast as she could, exceeding her acknowledged top speed of 14½ knots by three knots. Captain Rostron steered her skillfully through the maze of icebergs and from 3:00AM ordered rockets to be fired at 15-minute intervals so the survivors knew help was coming. An hour later, a green light was seen in the water some 300 yards ahead. It was lifeboat number two. Within 10 minutes, the 25 weary but relieved survivors, led by Fourth Officer Boxhall, began to make their way aboard the rescue ship. Ladders and nets were slung over the side for the men, while women were hauled up in slings and bosun's chairs and children in canvas bags. The nightmare was over ... for some.

Over the next four hours, survivors were taken aboard the *Carpathia*. The last to be rescued were the 70-plus in lifeboat number 12, which was under the command of Second Officer Lightoller. With the boat sagging low in the water under the weight of numbers, Lightoller was worried that they might not be spotted by *Carpathia* and had to sound several sharp blasts on his seaman's whistle to attract attention. Finally, the alarms were heeded and at 8:30AM the small boat drew alongside the liner. Lightoller himself was at the very back of the line to climb the ladder — the last man from the *Titanic* to be plucked to safety.

The *Carpathia's* passengers lined the deck in silence as the survivors clambered aboard. They were the first outsiders to realize the full extent of the tragedy. Captain Rostron ordered a headcount of those picked up safely from the *Titanic* and came up with a figure of 705. The official White Star list published on April 20 calculated 757 survivors, while the British Court of Inquiry gave 711. However, nobody can be sure exactly how many people were rescued or how many were on board when the

Titanic went down. In round figures, it is accepted that there were more than 2,200 on board, of whom more than 1,500 were lost.

What is certain is that those in first-class fared considerably better than those in steerage. According to the British Report, 62 per cent of first-class passengers aboard the *Titanic* were saved; 41 per cent of second-class; 38 per cent of third-class; and just 24 per cent of crew.

Not wishing to alarm the families of those who had sailed on the *Titanic*, Captain Rostron imposed a news blackout on the disaster. This resulted in distortion and confusion. Early newspaper reports indicated that everyone on board had been saved, thus giving false hope to the very people whom Rostron wanted to protect. Only the *Titanic's* sister ship, the *Olympic*, was furnished with information and it was not until 6:16PM New York time on the Monday that Captain Haddock of the *Olympic* was able to confirm the sinking to White Star: "*Carpathia* reached *Titanic's* position at daybreak. Found boats and wreckage only. *Titanic* had foundered about 2:20AM in 41°46'N, 50°14'W. All her boats accounted for. About 675 souls saved, crew and passengers, latter nearly all women and children. Leyland Line S.S. *Californian* remaining and searching position of disaster. *Carpathia* returning to New York with survivors; please inform Cunard. Haddock."

As the *Carpathia* headed towards New York, her progress slowed by the sheer volume of passengers, the world besieged her for news of survivors. Harold Bride, who had to be carried up from the dispensary where he was being treated for frostbite, was persuaded to join Harold Cottam in the wireless room. Cottam had not slept for nearly 30 hours. Their task was to transmit the list of survivors to the outside world via a land station on top of Wanamaker's Department Store in New York where

"WOMEN AND CHILDREN FIRST"
For many survivors, this was the abrupt end to their family lives and treasured relationships.

messages were received by 21-year-old operator David Sarnoff. Meanwhile, Bride and Cottam ignored all other pleas for information, whatever the source. Even a personal request from President Taft regarding the safety of his friend Archie Butt remained unanswered.

Back at the disaster site, the *Californian*, under her captain, Bolton-born Stanley Lord, searched in vain for survivors. The *Californian*'s belated appearance on the scene has subsequently cast her as the villain of the piece by those who believe that she was in a position to save many of those killed. Had she

EYEWITNESS

Alfred White, a greaser in the engine-room, described the situation below.

"I was on the whale deck in the bow calling the watch that was to relieve me when the ice first came aboard. The collision opened the seams below the water-line but did not even scratch the paint above the line. I know that because I was one of those who helped to make an examination over the side with a lantern. I went down into the engine-room at 12:40AM. We even made coffee, so there was not much thought of danger. An hour later I was still working at the light engines. I heard the chief engineer tell one of his subordinates that number six bulkhead had given way. At that time things began to look bad ... I was told to go up and see how things were, and made my way up a dummy funnel to the bridge deck. By that time all the boats had left the ship, yet everyone in the engine-room was at his post. I was near the captain and heard him say, 'Well boys, it's every man for himself now.'"

MOMENT OF SEPARATION

"The men stood away and waited in absolute silence ... The boats were then swung out and lowered."

been the mystery ship seen from the bridge of the *Titanic*?

A cargo vessel of 6,223 tons and with a design speed of around 13 knots, the *Californian* was built in Dundee, Scotland, in 1901-2, for the Leyland Line of Liverpool. She left Liverpool on April 5, 1912, bound for Boston, carrying a mixed cargo but no passengers. Aware of ice in the vicinity on the evening of the 14th, Captain Lord doubled his lookouts at 8:00PM. Two and a quarter hours later, he saw what he thought was the glow of ice ahead and, at 10:21PM, he ordered the engines to be stopped and the helm to be swung hard a-port so that she faced north-east. With his ship surrounded by loose ice, Lord decided to stay put for the night in a position he worked out as 42°5'N, 50°7'W. Using the calculations of Fourth Officer Boxhall on the *Titanic*, this meant that the *Californian* was no more than 20 miles north of the *Titanic*, when it struck the iceberg.

On leaving the bridge, Lord spotted a light to the east, which he presumed to be an approaching vessel. He saw it again shortly afterwards and asked whether there were any other ships in the area. Wireless operator Cyril Evans replied, "Only *Titanic*."

But Lord did not think the light belonged to *Titanic* — he thought it was a smaller ship. "You'd better contact *Titanic* anyway," he told Evans, "and let her know we're stopped in ice." Evans did, but was cut off by Jack Phillips before being able to give the exact position. Having been on duty since 7:00AM, Evans decided to go to bed. Just when *Titanic* was to need her most, the *Californian* was uncontactable by radio.

By 11:30PM, the other ship's green starboard light was visible some five miles away, according to Lord, but all attempts to contact her by Morse lamp were in vain. At midnight, Second Officer Herbert Stone took over as officer of the watch. He believed the ship to be a small tramp steamer. Fireman Ernest Gill went on deck around midnight and, confusingly, saw a vessel that he described as a very large steamer, about 10 miles away, going at full speed. Forty minutes later, Gill saw a white rocket from approximately the same position, followed by

another, seven or eight minutes later. "I thought it must be a shooting star," he stated subsequently. "It was not my business to notify the bridge or the lookouts ... I turned in immediately after."

Second Officer Stone also saw flashes of white light in the sky — five in all. To him, they seemed to be coming from an area beyond the unidentified ship. At 1:15AM, he reported his observations to Captain Lord, who urged him to continue signaling by Morse lamp. Again there was no reply. While Lord tried to rest, apprentice James Gibson joined Stone on the upper bridge. Focussing his binoculars on the distant ship, Gibson saw a sixth rocket — a white flash followed by a series of white stars. Two more followed quickly, the last at 1:40AM. The pair discussed the implications. "A ship is not going to fire rockets at sea for nothing," observed Stone. Gibson agreed, wondering whether it was a sign of "some sort of distress." They then noticed the ship appeared to be listing to starboard and that the glare of lights on her afterdeck looked higher than before. "She seems to look queer now," remarked Stone. Gibson answered, "She looks rather to have a big side out of the water." At around 2:00AM, only the stern light of the other ship could be seen. Stone said she was changing course and beginning to steam away to the south-west, yet there was no sign of her green light, which should have been visible if she had been heading in that direction. Gibson later testified that he thought she had disappeared at 2:05AM, but Stone said she was still just visible until 2:20AM, at which point her lights vanished. Had the disappearance of this strange ship been caused by her sinking, not her departure? Had Stone and Gibson been watching the death throes of the *Titanic*?

Stone told Gibson to wake Captain Lord and to inform him that the other ship had fired eight white rockets. Lord later said that, in his drowsy state, he had no recollection of being given this information. All he remembered was Gibson opening the door and closing it immediately.

Two and a half hours later, as dawn broke on the *Californian*, a four-masted steamer with one yellow funnel was visible eight miles away. Reminded of the

"I thought it must be a shooting star. It was not my business to notify the bridge or the lookouts."

☆

EYEWITNESS

Eight-year-old Marshall Drew, traveling with his Uncle Jim and Aunt Lulu, remembered every detail of the fateful night right up until his death in 1986.

"When the Titanic struck the iceberg, I was in bed. However, for whatever reason I was awake and remember the jolt and cessation of motion. A steward knocked on the stateroom door and directed us to get dressed, put on life preservers and go to the boat deck, which we did ... the steward as we passed was trying to arouse passengers who had locked themselves in for the night. Elevators were not running. We walked up to the boat deck. All was calm and orderly. An officer was in charge. 'Women and children first,' he said, as he directed lifeboat number 11 to be filled. There were many tearful farewells. We and Uncle Jim said good-bye ... The lowering of the lifeboat 70 feet to the sea was perilous. Davits, ropes, nothing worked properly, so that first one end of the lifeboat was tilted up and then far down. I think it was the only time I was scared. Lifeboats pulled some distance away from the sinking Titanic, afraid of what suction might do ... As row by row of the porthole lights of the Titanic sank into the sea this was about all one could see. When the Titanic upended to sink, all was blacked out until the tons of machinery crashed to the bow ... As this happened hundreds and hundreds of people were thrown into the sea. It isn't likely I shall ever forget the screams of these people as they perished in water said to be 28 degrees ... At this point in my life I was being brought up as a typical British kid. You were not allowed to cry. You were a 'little man.' So as a cool kid I lay down in the bottom of the lifeboat and went to sleep. When I awoke it was broad daylight as we approached the Carpathia. Looking around over the gunwale it seemed to me like the Arctic. Icebergs of huge size ringed the horizon for 360 degrees."

———— ☆ ————

French sculptor Paul Chevre spoke of the wait to be rescued.

"When our boat had rowed about half a mile from the vessel the spectacle was quite fairylike. The Titanic, which was fully illuminated, was stationary, like some fantastic piece of stage scenery. The night was clear and the sea smooth, but it was intensely cold. Presently the gigantic ship began to sink by the bows, and then those who had remained on board realized the horror of their situation. Suddenly the lights went out and an immense clamor filled the air in one supreme cry for help. Little by little the Titanic settled down, and for three hours cries of anguish were heard. At moments the cries of terror were lulled and we thought it was all over, but the next instant they were renewed in still keener accents. As for us we did nothing but row, row, row to escape from the death cries. In our little boat we were frozen with cold, having left the ship without overcoats or rugs. We shouted from time to time to attract attention, but obtained no reply. A German baron who was with us fired off all the cartridges in his revolver. This agonizing suspense lasted for many hours until at last the Carpathia appeared. We shouted 'Hurrah!' and all the boats scattered on the sea made towards her."

rockets seen in the night, Captain Lord became concerned that the ship might be in difficulty (even though it was a different ship from that seen earlier) and ordered Evans to try to contact her by radio. No sooner had Evans turned on his set than the German steamer *Frankfurt* advised him that *Titanic* had sunk three hours ago. Armed with *Titanic*'s last known location, Evans informed his captain, who immediately ordered the engines to be started up and the crew alerted. The *Californian* shuddered into motion just after 6:00AM and, slowed by the ice, reached the *Titanic*'s stated position some 90 minutes later. However there was no sign of any wreckage or lifeboats and it was not until *Carpathia* was spotted and contacted by wireless that the *Californian* was able to offer genuine assistance. But by then there was little to be done.

Landing the survivors and burying the dead

While the *Californian* conducted a futile search for survivors, the *Carpathia* plowed through fog and thunderstorms on her way to New York, arriving

there on the evening of Thursday April 18. By now, the world's press was aware of the scale of the disaster and crowds had been besieging the White Star offices in New York and Southampton, desperate for news. But many of the names relayed from the *Carpathia* were vague and incorrect, bearing little similarity to anyone on board. Friends and relatives would only believe their loved ones were safe when they actually saw them in the flesh.

Consequently, more than 10,000 gathered to greet the *Carpathia* as it docked, the numbers boosted by early exponents of check-book journalism, eager to buy exclusives. As the battle-weary survivors flopped into welcoming arms on the dock, the different classes once again went their separate ways. First-class passengers, such as the newly widowed Mrs. Charles Hays, Mrs. George Widener, and the Thayers, departed on private

ORDEAL OVER *When the last of the* **Titanic's** *lifeboats was picked up by the* **Carpathia,** *it had been drifting in freezing seas for nine hours.*

trains. Others stayed at the city's finest hotels. Meanwhile, the third-class survivors, many of whom had lost everything in the disaster, trudged ashore with the prospect of nowhere to sleep for the night. Happily, White Star provided temporary shelter.

Back out in the frozen waters of the North Atlantic, the grim task of retrieving bodies was undertaken by the cable ship *Mackay-Bennett*, which had set out from Halifax, Nova Scotia, carrying tons of ice, more than 100 coffins, 40 embalmers, and an Anglican canon to conduct burials at sea. The ship arrived at the scene at 8:00PM on Saturday April 20. Fifty-one bodies were recovered on the first day, including a two-year-old boy, whose entry in the ledger read simply, "No identification. No effects."

After more than five days in the sea, many of the bodies had deteriorated. Those with distinguishing features or property were embalmed and brought back to Halifax in the hope that they could be identified, but 24, who were disfigured beyond recognition, were weighted into sacks and buried at sea.

With three other ships arriving to lend assistance, the search for the dead continued for six weeks. A total of 328 bodies were found, of which 128 were unrecognizable. The vast majority of these (119) were buried at sea, but the small boy was returned to Halifax, where he was buried as "the unknown child." Subsequent research indicates that he was probably Gosta Leonard Paulson, who had sailed from Southampton with his mother, two sisters and brother, all of whom were lost.

One body that was easily identifiable was number 124 — John Jacob Astor. His shirt had his initials in the collar. His effects included a gold watch, gold cuff links with diamonds, a diamond ring with three stones, £225 in English bank notes, $2,440, £5 in gold, 50 francs, and a gold pencil.

RACE AGAINST TIME
The Carpathia exceeded her top speed and had to navigate seas strewn with icebergs to reach the Titanic's last radioed position.

EYEWITNESS

Colonel Archibald Gracie jumped from the top deck of the Titanic and was sucked down with her.

"After sinking with the ship, it appeared to me as if I was propeled by some great force through the water. This might have been occasioned by explosions under the water, and I remembered fearful stories of people being boiled to death. Again and again I prayed for deliverance, although I felt sure that the end had come. I had the greatest difficulty in holding my breath until I came to the surface. I knew that once I inhaled, the water would suffocate me. When I got under water I struck out with all my strength for the surface. I got to air again after a time, which seemed to me to be unending. There was nothing in sight save the ocean, dotted with ice and strewn with large masses of wreckage. Dying men and women all about me were groaning and crying piteously. By moving from one piece of wreckage to another, at last I reached a cork raft. Soon the raft became so full that it seemed as if she would sink if more came on board her. The crew for self-preservation had therefore to refuse to permit any others to climb aboard. This was the most pathetic and horrible scene of all. The piteous cries of those around us still ring in my ears, and I will remember them to my dying day. 'Hold on to what you have, old boy!' we shouted to each man who tried to get on board. 'One more of you would sink us all!' Many of those whom we refused answered as they went to their death, 'Good luck — God bless you!'"

George Brayton was travelling first class.

"A number of us who were enjoying the crisp air were promenading about the deck. Captain Smith was on the bridge when the first cry from the lookout came that there was an iceberg ahead. It may have been 30 feet high when I saw it. It was possibly 200 yards away and dead ahead. Captain Smith shouted some orders ... a number of us promenaders rushed to the bow of the ship. When we saw he could not fail to hit it, we rushed to the stern. Then came a crash, and the passengers were panic-stricken."

Seaman Thomas Jones praised the courage of the Countess of Rothes in lifeboat number eight.

"I saw the way she was carrying herself and the quiet, determined manner in which she spoke, and I knew she was more of a man than most aboard, so I put her in command at the tiller. There was another woman in the boat who helped, and was every minute rowing. It was she who suggested we should sing, and we sang as we rowed, starting with 'Pull for the Shore.' We were still singing when we saw the lights of the Carpathia, and then we stopped singing and prayed."

AFTERMATH

The Carpathia's passengers joined her crew in helping the Titanic's lucky but distressed survivors.

Services for the dead were held in the United States, Britain and France. One of the true heroes to emerge from the disaster was bandleader Wallace Hartley and when his body was taken to his home town of Colne in Lancashire, people came from far and wide to pay tribute.

The official inquiries

As a more complete picture of the tragedy began to emerge, the question on everyone's lips was: How could it have happened? Those who had suffered a loss as a result were also demanding to know who was responsible, so a United States Senate investigation into the affair was hastily convened under the chairmanship of Michigan Republican Senator, William Alden Smith. Assisted by a committee, Smith opened the inquiry on April 19, just four days after the sinking of the *Titanic*.

The hearings lasted 17 days, with testimony and affidavits from witnesses filling 1,145 pages. The

IN CHARGE OF THE *CARPATHIA*
Captain Arthur Rostron (seated center) poses with his senior officers.

EYEWITNESS

English schoolmaster, Lawrence Beesley, was traveling in second class.

"As I dressed, I heard the order shouted, 'All the passengers on deck with life belts on.' We all walked up slowly with the life belts tied on over our clothing, but even then we presumed that this was merely a wise precaution the captain was taking. The ship was absolutely still, and except for the gentle, almost unnoticeable, tilt downwards, there were no visible signs of the approaching disaster. But, in a few moments, we saw the covers being lifted from the boats and the crews allotted to them standing by and uncoiling the ropes, which were to lower them. We then began to realize that it was a more serious matter than we had at first supposed. Presently we heard the order, 'All men stand back away from the boats. All ladies retire to the next deck below.' The men all stood away and waited in absolute silence, some leaning against the end railings of the deck, others pacing slowly up and down. The boats were then swung out and lowered. When they were level with the deck where all the women were collected, the women got in quietly, with the exception of some, who refused to leave their husbands. In some cases they were torn from their husbands and pushed into the boats, but in many instances they were allowed to remain, since there was no-one to insist that they should go."

CURTAILED TRIP

The **Carpathia** *had been en route to the Mediterranean when she heard the* **Titanic's** *distress call. After picking up survivors, she immediately returned to New York.*

first witness was J. Bruce Ismay, already seen by many as the ideal scapegoat, on the basis that he had managed to escape in a lifeboat while so many had perished. The jingoistic New York *American* newspaper published a photograph of Ismay surrounded by pictures of victims' widows. The headline left little room for misinterpretation: "J. BRUTE ISMAY."

Although visibly exhausted, Ismay insisted that he had "nothing to hide" and proceeded to allay rumors that the *Titanic* had been trying for a record crossing. When asked how he had succeeded in finding a place in a lifeboat when so many of his company's customers — women and children included — had failed, he replied, "The boat was there. There was a certain number of men in the boat, and the officer called out asking if there were any more women, and there were no passengers on the deck. As the boat was in the act of being lowered away, I got into it."

Ismay also defended himself against accusations that he had demanded the best cabin on the rescue ship *Carpathia*. "When I got on board the ship I stood with my back against the bulkhead, and somebody came up and said, 'Will you not go into the saloon and get some soup or something to drink?'... 'No,' I said, 'I really do not want anything at all... If you will get me in some room where I can be quiet, I wish you would.'... Then he took me and put me into a room. I did not know whose the room was, at all." The room he had been given belonged to the ship's doctor.

Among the 82 witnesses called were Second Officer Lightoller, Fourth Officer Boxhall, lookout Frederick Fleet, Guglielmo Marconi, and Captain Lord. One of the most controversial witnesses was steward George Crowe, who told the inquiry, "There were various men passengers, probably Italians, or some foreign nationality other than English or American, who attempted to rush the boats." When Fifth Officer Harold Lowe also used "Italian" as a synonym for "coward," he was obliged to apologize to the Italian ambassador in the US.

Although severely critical of Captain Smith, Senator Smith paid fulsome tribute to the career of his namesake. "Captain Smith," he said, "knew the sea and his clear eye and steady hand had often guided his ship through dangerous paths. For forty years, storms sought in vain to vex him or menace his craft ... Each new advancing type of ship built by his company was handed over to him as a reward for faithful services and as evidence of confidence in his skill. Strong of limb, intent of purpose, pure in character, dauntless as a sailor could be, he walked the deck of this majestic structure as master of her keel." Continuing in this eloquent vein, Senator Smith added that the Captain's "own willingness to die was the expiating evidence of his fitness to live."

The final day of the inquiry was May 25, by which time the abrasive Senator Smith, who had asked virtually all the questions, had been dismissed as a buffoon by the American press. He presented his report to the Senate three days later. He castigated the British Board of Trade over the shortage of lifeboats, Captain Smith for his "indifference to danger, overconfidence and neglect to heed the oft-repeated warnings of his friends" and, most scathingly of all, Captain Lord for his failure to act. The report said, "The committee is forced to the inevitable conclusion that the *Californian*, controlled by the same company, was nearer the *Titanic* than the 19 miles reported by her captain, and that her officers and crew saw the distress signals of the

THE GRIM NEWS BREAKS
... but not immediately. Early reports from White Star suggested that the **Titanic** *was afloat and being towed to port.*

HERO'S FAREWELL
The story of Wallace Hartley captured the public imagination. Crowds flocked to his funeral at Colne in Lancashire to pay their last respects.

Titanic and failed to respond to them in accordance with the dictates of humanity, international usage and the requirements of law." This had been "most reprehensible" and Lord had incurred "a grave responsibility."

Praising Captain Rostron, the report made two major recommendations — that lifeboat capacity be increased to a place for each person aboard and that wireless equipment should be manned for 24 hours.

The British Court of Inquiry convened for the first time on May 2 under the auspices of Wreck Commissioner Lord Mersey. A large model of the

stricken ship was built to help Lord Mersey and his team of five assessors visualize events on the night in question. The Board of Trade, represented by the Attorney General, Sir Rufus Isaacs, drew up a list of 26 questions to be answered by the court. These concerned the construction of the *Titanic*, navigation, ice warnings received on the night and the proximity of the *Californian*. By the time the jury retired on June 21, the testimony had amounted to 25,622 questions and answers.

Crew members on both the *Titanic* and the *Californian* gave their version of events and Marconi was again questioned about the role of wireless in maritime safety. Ismay repeated his assertion that he had no control whatsoever over the speed of the *Titanic*, a statement supported by Captain Rostron, who said that no captain — least of all Smith — would take orders from anybody while at sea. When pressed about the ice warning that he had stuffed into his pocket, Ismay tried to absolve himself of any blame and attempted to justify Captain Smith's decision not to reduce speed. Ismay tied himself in a verbal knot, but his version was accepted. As he insisted, he was not a navigator.

Another to receive a rough ride was Sir Cosmo Duff Gordon, who was accused of bribery, but he too managed to satisfy the commissioners on that count, although they did criticize him for not imploring the crew of his lifeboat to go back and rescue the dying. In the end, the commission exonerated both Ismay and Duff Gordon, to the annoyance of the American press, who had been hoping to lay at least part of the blame at the door of the British aristocracy. Of Ismay, Lord Mersey said, "Had he not jumped in he would merely have added one more life, namely his own, to the number of those lost."

Lord Mersey attached little relevance to the question of the missing binoculars. In doing so, he was echoing the views of the explorer Sir Ernest Shackleton who had been called as an expert witness. Shackleton argued that binoculars were no substitute for the naked eye. Binoculars, he said, tended to localize the vision whereas a watchful pair of eyes could take in the whole horizon. "I do not believe in any lookout man having glasses at all," added Shackleton. "I only believe in the officer using them, and then only when something has been reported in a certain quarter or a certain place on the bow." In view of this evidence, it was no surprise when Lord Mersey stated: "The judgment is that binoculars are not desirable in the crow's nest." Good eyesight was deemed infinitely more valuable.

The commission ruled that the loss of the *Titanic* "was due to collision with an iceberg, brought about by the excessive speed at which she was being navigated." However, it cleared Captain Smith of negligence, deciding that he was merely following custom by not slowing down for ice warnings in clear weather. "I am told," said Lord Mersey, "that it is not the practice to find negligence against a dead man. He has no opportunity of giving any explanation." The inquiry had heard other captains testify how they were willing to plow

IN LOVING MEMORY *Wallace Hartley's grave.*

CLAIMS

The National Sailors' and Firemen's Union provided shipwreck pay to surviving members of the Titanic's *crew.*

A total of $16,804,112 (£3,464,765) was submitted in claims for loss of life and property resulting from the sinking of the *Titanic*. The largest claim was made by the baggage-laden Mrs. Charlotte Drake Cardeza, who filed a 14-page claim against White Star for loss of personal property totaling $177,352.75 (£36,567).

Other claims included:

Hakan Bjornstrom-Steffanson (oil painting by Blondel, "La Circasienne Au Bain"): $100,000.

William Carter (one Renault 35 horse-power automobile): $5,000.

Eugene Daly (set of bagpipes): $50.

Robert W. Daniel (champion French bulldog, Gamin de Pycombe): $750.

Emilio Portaluppi (signed picture of Garibaldi): $3,000.

Edwina Troutt (marmalade machine): 8s 5d.

Ella Holmes White (four roosters and hens): $207.87.

through fog and ice in the belief that the faster they traveled through danger, the faster they escaped from it.

The Board of Trade also got off lightly. While acknowledging that the British lifeboat regulations were hopelessly out of date, the commission was impressed by the claim that the Board of Trade had been considering new safety rules even before the disaster. So who was to blame for this dreadful loss of life? Echoing the American report, Lord Mersey and his team attached much of the blame to the *Californian*. "I think we are all of the opinion that the distress rockets that were seen from the *Californian* were the distress signals of the *Titanic* ... She could have reached the *Titanic* if she had made the attempt when she saw the first rocket. She made no attempt."

The recommendations were that lifeboat capacity should be provided for everyone on board; lifeboat drill should be improved and enforced; ship construction should feature watertight decks, longitudinal bulkheads and high double bottoms; lookouts should have regular eye tests; wireless should be compulsory and manned around the clock; speed should be reduced in ice fields; and masters should be reminded that it was an offense not to help a ship in distress.

WITNESS
Second Officer Lightoller (center) was one of 82 survivors to give evidence to a Senate investigation into the disaster. A British Court of Inquiry was convened later.

Thus reputations were savaged and saved, blame apportioned and cleared. But if those involved thought that this marked the final investigation into the sinking of the *Titanic*, they were sorely mistaken. For this was a story that would run and run.

GUGLIELMO MARCONI
The manufacturer of the **Titanic's** *telegraphy also gave evidence.*

CHAPTER FOUR
THE LEGACY OF THE TITANIC

Even before the Mersey Commission had presented its report, film-makers were seeking to cash in on the dramatic story of the *Titanic*. After all, it had everything – heroic deeds, human interest, controversy and a vast loss of life. No Hollywood screenwriter could have dreamed up a more gripping tale.

TITANIC DISCOVERY *"It was incredible. All those years and all those efforts ... and BANG. There it was!"*

On May 14, 1912, just one month after the tragedy, actress Dorothy Gibson, one of the survivors of the disaster, co-wrote and starred in the silent movie *Saved from the Titanic*. The big business that was to surround the *Titanic* was underway.

Little did Dorothy Gibson know, but she could have had a truly happy ending to her film. For at least one romance had blossomed during the tragedy. First-class passengers Robert Daniel and Mary Eloise Smith survived, but Mary's husband, Lucien, died. Mrs. Smith and Daniel met on the rescue ship *Carpathia*, became friends and married within two years. And, in August 1912, the newly widowed Madeleine Astor gave birth to a son. She named him after her husband, who had acted with such dignity as the liner went down.

The fate of the principal players

In 1913, J. P. Morgan, the owner of the *Titanic* and a shadowy figure, died aged 76. In the same year, the racehorse Craganour was mysteriously disqualified after being first past the post in the English Derby. No other owner or jockey protested about the winner, but the stewards, acting on their own initiative, suddenly awarded the race to 100-1 runner Aboyeur, who had finished second. Everyone was puzzled until it emerged that Craganour was owned by one B. Ismay. In fact, it was Bower Ismay, Bruce's younger brother, but the widespread feeling was that English racing would not allow a horse owned by the Ismay family to win their most precious prize. Although he had been vindicated by the inquiry and had received a warm welcome on his return to Britain, J. Bruce Ismay's behavior aboard the *Titanic* had not been forgiven by some.

Ismay was never the same man following the sinking of the *Titanic*. Every newspaper or magazine account of the fateful night brought it all back to him. He retired as chairman of the White Star Line in June 1913 and, although continuing to serve on a number of boards, preferred to remain in the background. In the aftermath of the First World War, he sold his country home near Liverpool and began spending an increasing amount of time on his estate, The Lodge,

DOROTHY GIBSON
Her ordeal on the **Titanic** *led swiftly to a starring role.*

at Costelloe, County Galway, on the west coast of Ireland. Although his public profile was now considerably lower than it had been in the years before the disaster, he continued to attend concerts in London and to hunt and fish in Scotland. Further misfortune befell him when The Lodge was

KINEMATOGRAPH WEEKLY
June 26, 1958

A TITANIC PICTURE THAT WILL BRING YOU TITANIC FIGURES...

TRADE SHOWS

LONDON: Odeon, Leicester Square, Friday, June 27th

GLASGOW	Odeon	Tues.	July 1st
NEWCASTLE	Odeon	Wed.	July 2nd
LEEDS	Odeon	Thurs.	July 3rd
SHEFFIELD	Odeon	Fri.	July 4th
CARDIFF	Capitol	Tues.	July 8th
BIRMINGHAM	West End	Wed.	July 9th
LIVERPOOL	Odeon	Thurs.	July 10th
MANCHESTER	Odeon	Fri.	July 11th

All the above Trade Shows commence at **10.30 a.m.**

THE RANK ORGANISATION PRESENTS

KENNETH MORE IN A NIGHT TO R[...]

FROM THE BOOK BY WALTER LORD · SCREENPLAY BY ERIC AMBLER · PRODUCED BY WILLIAM MacQUITTY · DI[...]

"A NIGHT TO REMEMBER"
Ruislip Reservoir stood in for the cruel Atlantic in the lifeboat scenes.

mysteriously destroyed by fire but he supervised the rebuilding and enjoyed entertaining his grandchildren there during the summer holidays. Ismay retired from business in 1934 and two years later was confined to a wheelchair after a circulatory illness had necessitated the amputation of his right leg. His health in general began to deteriorate and he eventually died from a stroke on October 17, 1937.

White Star also ensured that no officer from the

EXECUTIVE PRODUCER EARL ST. JOHN

MEMBER

BY ROY BAKER   RANK FILM DISTRIBUTORS LTD

his remaining years in retirement in his native Wales. Lightoller also served in the Navy before rejoining White Star where he was appointed Chief Officer of the *Celtic*. Repeatedly overlooked for promotion, he retired in the early 1920s to run a chicken farm. He had one final brush with fame in 1940 when his yacht *Sundowner* formed part of the fleet of "little ships" at Dunkirk. Once again rising to the occasion, he single-handedly rescued 131 British soldiers from the clutches of the Germans.

And what of the other principal players in the tragedy? Unlike J. Bruce Ismay, Sir Cosmo Duff Gordon was determined to put on a brave face. He heard all the jibes but, in public at least, adopted the traditional British stiff upper lip. In private, it was a different matter. Lady Duff Gordon said that the derision to which her husband was subjected "well nigh broke his heart." He died in 1931.

The other alleged "villain of the piece," Captain Stanley Lord, was forced to resign from the Leyland Line in August 1912. His ship did not last much longer — the *Californian* was sunk by a German submarine in 1917 (the *Carpathia* met a similar fate the following year). Lord was able to obtain a command with the London-based Nitrate Producers Steam Ship Company Ltd and remained there for 14 years, until his retirement in 1927. In the immediate aftermath of the Mersey Commission report, he had tried to clear his name, but when his efforts proved unsuccessful, he decided to let the matter rest. But the 1958 film about the *Titanic* sinking, *A Night To Remember*, reopened old wounds and once more Captain Lord set about proving his innocence. He enlisted the help of W. Leslie Harrison, general secretary of the British Mercantile Marine Service Association, who began seeking out fresh evidence in a bid to convince the Board of Trade to reconsider its condemnation of Lord. Right up until his death in 1962, Captain Lord maintained that, even if he had been aware that the *Titanic* was sinking, he would have been unable to steer the *Californian* through the ice field in time to pick up any survivors. After all, it had taken the *Carpathia* two and a half hours in daylight. Captain Lord resented Lord Mersey's

The report claimed that the Samson saw what turned out to be the ailing Titanic.

☆

Titanic ever achieved his own command. Even stalwarts such as Lightoller and Lowe were destined for declining careers. Lowe was appointed Third Officer on the downmarket *Medic* and, after serving in the Royal Navy during the First World War, spent

assertion that the *Californian* could have reached the *Titanic* without risk and could have saved the lives of most, if not all, of those on board. The sense of injustice was compounded by the fact that Captain Lord was called only as a witness at the British inquiry and as such was not given the opportunity to defend himself against the allegations.

Undeterred by Lord's death, Harrison forged ahead. It was widely accepted that other ships had been in the vicinity of the *Titanic* when she went down, but the identity of at least one remained a mystery until 1962, when a confidential 50-year-old report from Hendrik Naess, the first officer of the Norwegian vessel *Samson*, was finally made public. The report, originally made to the Norwegian authorities, claimed that the *Samson* saw what turned out to be the ailing *Titanic* and her distress rockets, but did not rush to her aid because the *Samson* had been engaged in illegal seal-hunting off south-east Canada. The master thought the rockets might have come from a fisheries-protection vessel, signaling a warning to the *Samson*. Rather than wait

to find out (the *Samson* had no wireless), the ship changed course and scurried away to the north. Was the *Samson* the mystery ship that was spotted from the ailing *Titanic*?

In 1965, Leslie Harrison presented a petition to the Board of Trade, but it was rejected. He tried again three years later, but met with the same response. This was despite the fact that Harrison was able to present fresh evidence at the second petition in the form of the observations of survivor Lawrence Beesley. The author of *The Loss of the Titanic*, generally regarded as the best eyewitness account of the sinking, Beesley had not been asked to testify at either of the official inquiries. In 1963, he had made an affidavit concerning the timing and number of the distress rockets fired from the *Titanic*. He said he had seen "about eight distress rockets fired," adding: "I left the ship in No. 13 lifeboat and I am quite confident that the last of these rockets had been fired before this lifeboat cleared *Titanic*'s side after being lowered into the water."

MELODRAMA
Most films on this subject play on the audience's emotions, such as in this scene from **Titanic 1953.**

TITANIC CAMEOS

The *Titanic* has made guest appearances in a number of movies and TV series:

1965 In the first episode of Irwin Allen's science fiction adventure *The Time Tunnel*, scientists James Darren and Robert Colbert try to change the course of history when they land on the deck of the *Titanic*.

1973 In the British period TV drama *Upstairs, Downstairs*, Lady Bellamy sails to her death on the *Titanic*.

1981 1981 Terry Gilliam's movie *Time Bandits* features a journey through time and space taking a schoolboy and his pals to such settings as Napoleonic France, Ancient Rome and the deck of the *Titanic*.

1989 The film *Ghostbusters II* sees the *Titanic* return as a ghost ship, complete with spooky passengers.

The ship has also played a part in novels. Danielle Steele's romantic blockbuster, *No Greater Love*, opens with the sinking of the *Titanic* and Jack Finney's 1995 novel, *From Time to Time*, places a time traveler on board the doomed liner in search of Major Archibald Butt.

The various attempts to find out exactly what happened on the night of April 14, 1912, ensured that interest in the Titanic never waned.

☆

Lifeboat 13 had left the *Titanic* at around 1:30AM yet the crew of the *Californian* insisted that they had witnessed rockets being fired right up until 2:00AM. Even taking into account the 12-minute time difference experienced by the two ships, the discrepancy appeared sufficient to cast new doubts as to whether the distress rockets seen by the *Californian* were actually those which had been fired from the *Titanic*.

For some reason, Lawrence Beesley had asked that his evidence should not be made public until after his death. When Beesley died in 1967 at the age of 89, Leslie Harrison was finally able to include details of the sworn statement in a petition on behalf of Captain Lord. Yet the Board of Trade rejected Beesley's evidence on the grounds that it was "not evidence that could not have been produced at the inquiry." It would be another 24 years before Captain Lord's role in proceedings would again come under close scrutiny.

You've read the book ...

The various attempts to find out exactly what happened on the night of April 14, 1912, ensured

that interest in the *Titanic* never waned. From the outset, books had appeared in droves, many offering a different interpretation on events and personalities. Following that early silent film, surprisingly it was another 30 years before the next *Titanic* movie appeared — and, even more surprisingly, it came from Germany. The 1943 film *Titanic* was a typical example of wartime Nazi propaganda, calculated to discredit British and Jewish businesses. A personal project of propaganda chief Josef Goebbels, it was directed by Herbert Selpin and showed the hero of the hour to be the only German on board. The character was purely fictional.

Hollywood endeavored to redress the balance in 1953 with Twentieth Century Fox's *Titanic*, starring Clifton Webb, Barbara Stanwyck, and Robert Wagner. Produced and co-written by Charles Brackett, it promised to recount "the greatest sea drama of all time." The model ship used to re-create the *Titanic* is now on display at the Marine Museum in Fall River, Massachusetts.

Two years later, author Walter Lord published his epic account of the *Titanic* disaster, *A Night To Remember*. Lord's publisher advised him against

ONCE THEY SAID GOD HIMSELF COULDN'T SINK HER. NOW THEY SAY NO MAN ON EARTH COULD RAISE HER.

RAISE THE TITANIC

LORD GRADE presents
a MARTIN STARGER PRODUCTION
JASON ROBARDS RICHARD JORDAN DAVID SELBY ANNE ARCHER
and ALEC GUINNESS in
RAISE THE TITANIC
Executive Producer MARTIN STARGER Screenplay by ADAM KENNEDY
Produced by WILLIAM FRYE Directed by JERRY JAMESON Music by JOHN BARRY
Adaptation by ERIC HUGHES Based on the Novel by CLIVE CUSSLER
FILMS INTERNATIONAL

"RAISE THE TITANIC"
Impresario Lord Grade had to raise £35 million to produce it. Audiences were unimpressed.

calling the book *Titanic*, lest such a title be jinxed. The book captured the public's imagination, introducing the story of the sinking to a whole new generation, and it was little surprise when it was turned into a film (Waddingtons even produced a 470-piece jigsaw to commemorate the event). Produced by William Macquitty for the British Rank Organisation and directed by Roy Baker, the film of *A Night To Remember* starred Kenneth More as Second Officer Charles Lightoller, David McCallum as wireless operator Harold Bride, and Alec McCowen as his counterpart on the *Carpathia*, Harold Cottam. Unlike the Hollywood version, it was more concerned with action than romance, although

the lifeboat scenes were shot at land-locked Ruislip reservoir near Pinewood Studios. Advertised as "an incredible, spellbinding story of six hours unlike any other six hours the world has ever known," the film was well received. The *New York Times* called it "a tense, exciting, and supremely awesome drama." But the film angered Captain Stanley Lord (no relation to Walter Lord) who was upset by the implication that the *Californian* just stood by while the *Titanic* sank.

In 1960, the musical *The Unsinkable Molly Brown* (based on the story of the gallant Denver millionairess, who had died in 1932) opened on Broadway in the United States. Four years later, this was also made into a movie, with Debbie Reynolds in the title role.

The petitions to the Board of Trade meant that the *Titanic* remained in public consciousness throughout the 1960s. There were other landmarks, too. In addition to the death of Lawrence Beesley, lookout Frederick Fleet, the first person to spot the iceberg, died in Southampton in 1965 at the age of 76. In his later years, Fleet had sold newspapers on the town's street corners.

New depths

The fascination with the *Titanic* resurfaced in 1977 with the publication of Clive Cussler's bestseller *Raise the Titanic!* Impresario Lord Grade was so captivated by the idea that he bought the film rights. Athens was hired to play New York and a rusty old liner called the *Athinai* played the newly raised *Titanic*. When a genuine Russian liner docked at Athens in the course of filming, her captain was more than a little alarmed to see the place swimming with American flags. Three years and $56 million later (Grade joked that it would have been cheaper to lower the Atlantic), *Raise the Titanic!* hit the big screen starring Jason Robards, Richard Jordan, and Alec Guinness. It was a resounding flop. *Variety* wrote, "It hits new depths hitherto unexplored by the worst of Lew Grade's overloaded ark melodramas. This one wastes a potentially intriguing premise with dull scripting, a lackluster cast, laughably phony trick work, and clunky direction that makes *Voyage of the Damned* seem inspired by comparison." The *Guardian* newspaper's reviewer was equally unimpressed: "The longer it all goes on, the more one hopes that, if they ever do raise the *Titanic*, they'll heave the film overboard to replace it."

The year before *Raise the Titanic!* sank without trace, the ship was the subject of a similarly lackluster American mini-series, *SOS Titanic*, featuring Cloris Leachman as Molly Brown and Helen Mirren as stewardess Mary Sloan.

Rumors of riches

Yet these offerings did nothing to dampen the spirits of *Titanic* aficionados worldwide. Back in 1958, the film *A Night To Remember* had fired the imagination of a group of young Americans. Led by 18-year-old Edward Kamuda, they went on to form a society of like-minded people called the Titanic Enthusiasts of America and produced their own journal, the *Titanic Communicator*. The society started with 45 subscribers but, now renamed the Titanic Historical Society, it boasts a membership of more than 3,000, drawn from such far-flung places as the United States, Britain, Australia, Germany, France, Holland, Norway, Hawaii, and Malaysia. (There are also separate *Titanic* societies in Britain and Norway.) Over the years, the THS has acquired a number of *Titanic* artifacts (a razor belonging to a steward, a ship's menu, Frederick Fleet's discharge book), but pride of place goes to the lifebelt worn by the pregnant Mrs. Madeleine Astor when she was rescued.

Members of the society also played their part in providing background information that led to the discovery that everyone with any interest in the legend of the great liner had been waiting for — the location of the wreck of the *Titanic*, discovered in 1985. The idea of finding and raising the *Titanic* from her ocean grave was hardly new and, since she rests in international waters, in theory anyone could dive for her. As long ago as March 1914, just two

years after the disaster, Denver architect Charles Smith drew up plans for raising the *Titanic* by using electromagnets and a submarine, but the project foundered because of lack of finance.

Although the passengers' insurance claims included only a few for items of jewelry (when it was clear that the ship would have to be evacuated, many of the ladies traveling in first-class had headed straight for the purser's office to reclaim their gems), rumors persisted that there were great riches to be found aboard the sunken wreck. Yet even the copy of *The Rubáiyát*, the *Titanic*'s most glittering treasure, had fetched only £405 ($625) when auctioned in London prior to its ill-fated voyage across the Atlantic. Nevertheless, encouraged either by old-fashioned romance or by sheer greed, a number of other would-be explorers concocted elaborate plans to bring the *Titanic* to the surface. Everyone thought they knew where the wreck was — from the ship's last known location — so all that was needed was manpower, technical expertise, and a lot of money.

Early attempts at salvage

Money, in particular, was in short supply until after the Second World War and so it was not until 1953 that the first serious attempt was made to locate the liner. In July of that year the British salvage vessel *Help* left Southampton bound for what was thought to be the *Titanic*'s position. Despite intensive underwater searches over a seven-day period, no trace of the *Titanic* was found. *Help* returned the following year, but again found nothing.

One man who was undeterred by the lack of success was Englishman Douglas Woolley. On the face of it, Woolley, who worked in a hosiery factory, had little to offer but an obsession with the lost liner. Almost annually between 1966 and 1977, he drew up plans for her salvage. They were all aborted, but his enthusiasm at least stirred interest among others who were able to generate the necessary financial backing.

Money was certainly no object to Texan oilman Jack Grimm. He had already sponsored expeditions in search of the Loch Ness Monster and Big Foot, so the *Titanic* was a natural progression. He enlisted the services of Columbia University's Lamont-Doherty Geological Observatory and, in July 1980, the expedition set out from Florida aboard the research vessel *H. J. W. Fay*. Once more, the results were disappointing. They tried again in the summers of 1981 and 1983, but came up with nothing conclusive, although Grimm maintained they had found the *Titanic*'s propeller. It later turned out to be a rock.

COURSE OF FATE
Distress calls from the Titanic *gave the liner's final position as 41°46'N 50°46'W. The wreck of the* Titanic *was found at 41°31'N 49°56'W.*

Success at last

The failure of these attempts disillusioned the press. It seemed that the precise location of the *Titanic* would remain unattainable forever. So when two scientific organizations, the French Institute for Research and Exploitation of the Seas (IFREMER) and the Woods Hole Oceanographic Institution of Massachusetts, announced that they were teaming

up for a new expedition, the venture attracted little publicity. Indeed it was a low-key affair, the prime objective being to conduct "deep-water engineering tests." Any discovery of the wreck of the *Titanic* would be a bonus.

Funded partly by the National Geographic Society, the voyage was led by Jean Jarry for the French and 42-year-old geologist Dr. Robert Ballard, the head of Woods Hole's Deep Submergence Laboratory. Born in Kansas, Ballard studied chemistry and geology at the University of California before gaining a Ph.D. in marine geology and geophysics at the University of Rhode Island. He subsequently joined Woods Hole, where his job entailed the exploration of the ocean floor. His interest in locating the *Titanic* dated back to the early 1970s, but at the time he was unable to attract financial support. Once he was working for the second largest oceanographic institution in the United States, however, things were different.

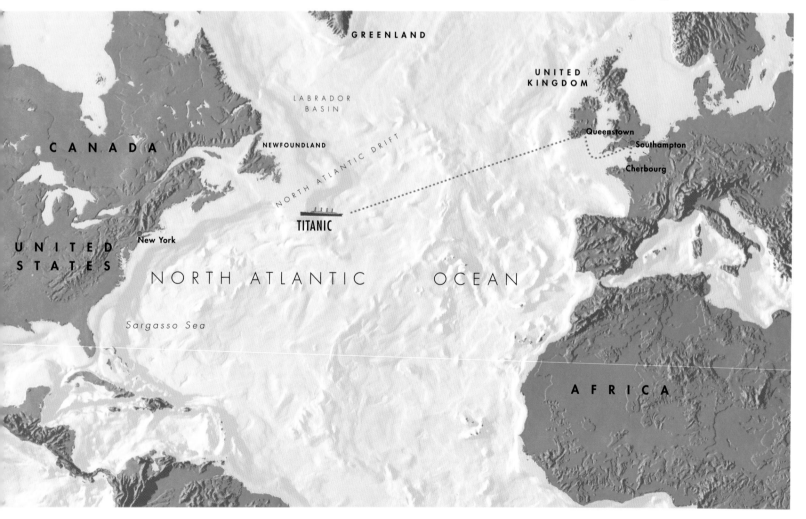

The equipment on this expedition included ARGO-Jason, a new American system designed to allow scientists to photograph the depths of the ocean without having to leave their surface vessel, and the French-developed SAR, a revolutionary side-scanning sonar, capable of examining the ocean floor in sweeps three-fifths of a mile wide.

Over a six-week period from the start of July 1985, the French research vessel *Le Suroit* began examining a 150 square mile area of sea, mainly to the south and east of *Titanic*'s last stated position, as Ballard was convinced that the failure of previous missions was because they had not searched a wide enough area. Some 80 per cent of the region was combed ("mowing the lawn" as the oceanographers called it), until *Le Suroit* ran out of time and returned home. It later transpired that at one point she had been just 100 yards away from success.

On August 22, her place was taken by the Woods Hole research vessel, *Knorr*, carrying 26 crew and 23 scientists. In tow, some 13,000 feet down, was the ARGO with its sonar system, powerful strobe lighting, and five television cameras pointing in different directions. One of its key attributes was that, unlike previous unmanned search and survey equipment, it could stay submerged for days at a time, if necessary.

Concentrating on the area not scanned by the French, the ARGO, under the watchful eyes of Ballard and engineer Jean-Louis Michel (with whom Ballard had worked in the past), scoured the ocean floor. For two weeks, there was absolutely no sign of *Titanic*'s presence, just a routine diet of mud punctuated by the occasional fish. Whenever the cameras found something dark, hopes would rise, only to be dashed on discovering that it was nothing more exciting than a large rock.

The night of August 31 offered more of the same. At midnight, Ballard's monitoring team was replaced by Michel's. While Ballard went below for a shower and some rest, Michel sat in the control room, closely observing the screens. Just before 1:00AM, he spotted something.

The cameras began picking up small chunks of metal. As the cameras panned along, it was clear that the objects were part of a trail of debris. Michel

THE ARGO
Working at a depth of 13,000 feet, this remote search and survey craft was to open the latest chapter in the Titanic's long story.

NORTH ATLANTIC BASIN
Among the many artifacts the ARGO discovered was this virtually unblemished ceramic bowl.

sent for Ballard who arrived just in time to see a large metal cylinder show up on screen. It was immediately identifiable as a boiler — but not just any boiler. Having studied photographs of the ship's mechanism for months beforehand, Ballard knew that this was a boiler from the *Titanic*.

Recalling the moment, he says, "It was incredible. All those years and all those efforts and days and days with the French and days and days before and BANG. There it was!"

The cameras set about following the trail to its natural conclusion. Some 600 yards along, they sent up pictures of a vast, dark object, which was clearly the *Titanic*. Formal identification would have to wait until the next day because Ballard was worried that the ARGO might become irretrievably entangled in the increasingly dense web of metal. In the meantime, aware that it was now around the same time of night as when the *Titanic* had sunk, Ballard arranged for a brief moment of silence to be observed in memory of those lost 73 years earlier.

Once daylight arrived, ARGO returned to the ocean floor. The large shadowy object was indeed the bow of the *Titanic*, sitting upright and in remarkably good condition with just a light covering of sediment. Such was the clarity of the pictures that every rivet was discernible, as were the heavy anchor chains, still in position, some of the passengers' lost luggage, a set of bedsprings, porcelain dishes, a tile from the first-class smoking room, a generator, a silver platter, a window from the second-class smoking room, a chamberpot, even bottles of wine (later identified as a Bordeaux and a Riesling), which had miraculously survived the disaster.

Then there was the crow's nest, with what seemed to be a telephone line hanging limply from it — the one through which Frederick Fleet had shouted that first warning about the iceberg.

The site of the wreck was pinpointed at 41°43'N, 49°56'W, although this was initially kept a secret to prevent opportunist looters from raiding the wreckage. Having found the bow, the *Knorr* spent the next five days scouring the area in search of the stern section, which had obviously broken off. Finally, on the fifth day, it was located in pieces some 2,000 feet behind the rest of the wreck. Two of the funnels, the

first and last, were missing. According to the account of Second Officer Lightoller, the forward funnel had crashed into the sea as the ship went down, very nearly killing him.

Back on dry land, Ballard, greeted by news teams from around the globe, gave a press conference. His concluding words were: "The *Titanic* itself lies in 13,000 feet of water on a gently sloping alpine-like countryside overlooking a small canyon below. Its bow faces north and the ship sits upright on the bottom. Its mighty stacks point upward. There is no light at this great depth and little light can be found. It is quiet and peaceful and a fitting place for the remains of this greatest of sea tragedies to rest. May it forever remain that way and may God bless these found souls."

WINDOWS AJAR
In April 1912, tons of freezing North Atlantic water would have crashed through these openings as the ship went down.

RESTING-PLACE
The ARGO's cameras found this wrought-iron bench standing eerily upright.

"A carnage of debris"

The following summer, Ballard returned to the site to conduct a more detailed investigation of the wreckage using yet more advanced camera technology. Probing the interior of the *Titanic*, the expedition found little more than a mass of debris where the luxurious staterooms had once been.

The "swimming eyeball," as the camera was nicknamed, is thought to have gone down as far as B deck. All of the wooden furnishings had vanished, eaten away over the decades by undersea worms. The steel columns which had supported the dome and staircase remained intact as did a number of crystal and brass light fittings, but the general picture was one of abject disarray. Up above, the wheelhouse had also been systematically devoured and all that was left of the wheel itself were the metal parts. The exploration came across the ship's safes. The arm of the robot approached the largest,

believed to have come from the second-class purser's office, and tugged at the handle but it refused to budge. Ballard recalled: "It had a big handle of bronze or gold, and we saw the dial. The door, with its beautiful crest, was polished and clean and looked brand new." There was an anxious moment when, on returning to the surface, the equipment accidentally brought up one of the *Titanic*'s steel cables. The team were determined not to disturb any part of the wreckage — "we thought the artifacts looked better exactly where they were," said Ballard — and the cable was immediately sent back into the water.

Scattered around the stern area were various items such as electric heaters, pots and pans and thousands of lumps of coal. Ballard was greatly relieved that there was no sign of any human remains. Even possessions were few and far between — a shoe here, a statue there and the head of a child's porcelain doll.

On account of the number of people who had met their deaths there, the stern section was the most traumatic area to work for Ballard and his team. Ballard described it as "a carnage of debris. It looked violent and torn, fragmented and jumbled like a rat's nest." He was keen to answer some of the puzzles still posed by the disaster, in particular about the precise nature of the damage caused by the iceberg. He found plenty of buckled plates, but the bow was buried 50 feet in debris and so the fatal gash could not be inspected. The only consolation, as Ballard saw it, was that the state of the *Titanic* would make it virtually impossible to salvage her.

Dr. Ballard's hope that the *Titanic* would be left to rest in peace proved to be over-optimistic. No sooner had the 1986 expedition returned home than enterprising privateers and government-backed organizations were laying plans to retrieve artifacts from the wreck. In July 1987, members of the French IFREMER Institute (who had fallen out with Ballard) teamed up with R.M.S. Titanic Inc. of New York to revisit the site. There they discovered a large hole in the starboard side of the bow, which was later attributed either to the explosion of the burning bunker or, more likely, to the impact of the bow on the ocean bed. They also retrieved some 1,800 artifacts — an act which aroused enormous controversy and accusations of grave-robbing. The United States Congress attempted to introduce a bill to prohibit the import of objects from the *Titanic*, but it fell by the wayside.

The results of the 1987 venture were put on display in museums in France and Scandinavia and included the ship's foremast bell, rudder indicator, a safe, plus quantities of silverplate and chinaware. A number of these were displayed on a French television show hosted by Telly Savalas, on which, amid much hype, the safe was opened and found to be empty. So much for the riches of the *Titanic*.

After fighting off a rival group, the Franco-American consortium returned to the wreckage in the summers of 1993 and 1994, making their total haul around 3,600 items. From October 1994, the National Maritime Museum in Greenwich staged an

A VIEW OF THE PANTRY
Some of the images sent back by the ARGO were poignantly evocative of life on board the great liner 73 years earlier.

WHEEL OF FORTUNE

The telemotor or "power steering" for the Titanic *is the only relic left from the bridge. The wooden wheel and casing are gone, but the part that remains is still a potent symbol for a ship which was heading toward a rendezvous with fate.*

exhibition of these artifacts, entitled "The Wreck of the *Titanic*." The exhibition was opened by William Macquitty, producer of *A Night To Remember*, and survivors Mrs. Edith Brown Haisman and Miss Millvina Dean who, at seven weeks old at the time of the disaster, was the youngest *Titanic* survivor. Among the items on display were the ship's telegraph, a steward's jacket, Major Arthur Peuchen's wallet (complete with contents), and the wrought-iron support of a wooden deck bench.

Although the exhibition proved tremendously popular with the public, concerns were expressed about its morality. Shortly before her death in 1996, survivor Eva Hart declared, "The ship is its own memorial. Leave it there." The museum, however, did not shy away from the controversy and was supported in its efforts by other survivors, including third-class passenger Beatrice Sandstrom. She told the museum, "I am personally pleased to see the *Titanic* story remembered by your fine efforts. Your presentation of the recovered objects from the ship

will help to teach the present and future generations the timeless human lessons learned from this great marine tragedy."

Reassessing the evidence

Supporters of the recovery efforts justified them by claiming that the expeditions would not only be preserving history but might also go some way towards solving some of the riddles surrounding the sinking of the *Titanic*. Dr. Ballard's discovery was certainly of great importance. It confirmed that, contrary to some eyewitness statements, the hull of the *Titanic* had broken as it plunged beneath the surface. The bow and stern sections were then separated, scattering their contents as they crashed to the ocean floor. The *Knorr* expedition had finally pinpointed the exact location of the *Titanic*, which turned out to be some 13 miles from the hasty estimate made by Joseph Boxhall shortly after the collision with the iceberg. In turn, this discrepancy cast new light on the supposed guilt of Captain Lord

TITANIC – NEW VENTURES

Virtual reconstructions of the Titanic's interior feature in a 3D video game.

Some of the latest *Titanic* projects include a 3D video game and a musical! The latter, opened on Broadway in April 1997 marking the 85th anniversary of the disaster. The musical includes upbeat songs and dancing...and a finale that takes place on a sloping stage. A major theme of the show, written by Peter Stone with music by Maury Yeston, is the contrast between the wealthy passengers on the upper decks and the poor immigrants down below.

The six principal characters are the builder, the owner, a passenger, a lookout, a stoker, and one of the radio operators. Maury Yeston says the musical is about dreams. "Immigrants dreamed of a better life in America," he says. "The middle class dreamed of becoming rich and the rich dreamed their dominance would last forever."

But his idea ran into early opposition. The Titanic Historical Society complained, "We don't think it is right. This was a terrible human tragedy. We don't see it as an event for jokes and singing."

Yeston admits the musical could have easily become the butt of cruel jibes. Before the first rehearsal, jokes were already sweeping theaterland. Among them was this prediction of a first-night review: "*Titanic* opened on Broadway last night...there were no survivors." In spite of the jokes, *Titanic* opened to incredible box office success. It also won five 1997 Tony Awards, including the prize for Best Musical.

and the *Californian*.

Confronted with this fresh information, the British Department of Transport agreed to reopen the 1912 inquiry that had condemned Lord without trial. After a two-year investigation, the department's report was published in March 1992, but it merely highlighted the differences in interpretation between the report's author, Captain James de Coverly, and Captain Thomas Barnett, who were given the task of reassessing the evidence. Barnett stood by the findings of the 1912 inquiry, which had concluded that the *Californian* was less than 10 miles from the *Titanic* at the time of the sinking. Captain de Coverly, however, put the distance between the two ships at 18 miles. Captain Barnett was sure that the ship that had been seen from the *Californian* that night was the *Titanic*, but Captain de Coverly believed it was a different vessel, most probably the Norwegian sealer *Samson*.

Captain de Coverly paid particular attention to the conduct of Herbert Stone, the *Californian*'s watch officer between midnight and 4:00AM on April 15, 1912. Stone did not exactly excel himself that night, sending an apprentice to inform the drowsy Captain Lord of the rockets rather than notifying the master

in person; failing to rouse wireless operator Evans when there was clearly a ship in distress; and failing to alert the engine room so that the *Californian* could swing into immediate action. Despite distributing a good deal of the blame in Stone's direction, Captain de Coverly did not clear Lord outright, stating that while it was unlikely that the *Californian* could have saved those lost on the *Titanic*, "an attempt should have been made." Thus the question of Captain Lord's culpability remains open to speculation.

The discovery of the wreck also cast doubts upon the strength and quality of the steel used in the *Titanic*'s hull. Samples from the 1987 expedition were brought back and analyzed by IFREMER and by the Canadian Bedford Institute of Oceanography. The results of these tests were announced in 1993 and suggested that the steel used in the *Titanic* and her sister ships became brittle when exposed to low water temperatures (when the *Titanic* struck the iceberg, the water temperature was down to around 31°F). Discussing "the real tragedy of *Titanic*," the paper concluded that "a better quality of steel plate might have averted her loss or resulted in an even slower rate of flooding that may have saved more crew and passengers." The samples also showed a

DR. ROBERT BALLARD

"In a word, sad" is how the man who discovered the wreck of the Titanic *views current attempts by others to raise it.*

high sulfur content — common in steel of that period — and this too rendered the metal more liable to fracture. The implication was clear — the *Titanic* was not the impregnable fortress she had been claimed to be.

The mission continues

Now that it has acquired exclusive salvage rights to the ship, R.M.S. *Titanic* is determined to raise at least part of her from the ocean bed. The latest attempt to do so took place in August 1996 before an audience of 1,700 tourists who had paid for the privilege. But it ended in disappointment, when the

cables lifting a 15-ton section of the *Titanic*'s hull suddenly snapped. The sea was not going to yield its treasures lightly.

R.M.S. president George Tulloch had mounted the £3.3 million operation to raise a section of the liner so that it could form the centerpiece for a New York exhibition on the *Titanic*. He was said to be close to tears when the mission had to be abandoned for another year.

There is sizable investment in the *Titanic* and the irrepressible Tulloch plans to sell trips to visit the wreck for $1,800 to $7,000, hoping to lure people with the promise that they will rub shoulders with

CONFETTI
This fragment of the hull is part of the center section of the boat which fell to pieces as the ship twisted and turned on its way to the bottom.

SOMBER REMINDERS

Some parts of the ship such as this bow railing are so easily recognizable that they are an eerie reminder of the fate of so many lost souls.

celebrities. He also hopes to sell off specially preserved, golfball-size chunks of *Titanic* coal for $25 apiece.

The Discovery cable TV channel is reportedly paying R.M.S. $3 million for film and TV rights and among the sponsors Tulloch has been wooing is the Bass brewery because he hopes to salvage 12,000 bottles of Bass Ale from the bottom of the ocean. He has also hinted that his company might be able to salvage Billy Carter's vintage Renault and the jeweled copy of *The Rubáiyát*.

But not everyone is keen for Tulloch to succeed. Karen Kamuda, vice-president of the Titanic Historical Society, thinks he is more concerned with making money than preserving history. The Society adds, "Most people who had relatives on board think this operation is gruesome and awful." When asked how he felt about the latest expedition, Dr. Robert Ballard replied, "In a word, sad."

Yet Tulloch is unrepentant. "The *Titanic* is not

easy to bring home," he admits. "But the greatest tragedy in the world is to give up. And we haven't given up. We'll get it next year."

The recent underwater interest in the *Titanic* has inevitably been reflected on dry land. A range of commemorative items was produced in 1989, including limited edition china plates and thimbles, both bearing pictures of the ship.

During the summer of 1991, a team of independent film-makers visited the wreck and produced a film, *Titanica*, which featured compelling footage of the sunken ship. The cameras revealed a macabre sight in the engine room — a pair of empty stoker's boots.

In the news again

In November 1996, CBS aired a four-hour TV mini-series entitled simply "*Titanic*." It starred George C. Scott as Captain Smith, Roger Rees as J. Bruce Ismay, Scott Hylands as John Jacob Astor, Janne Mortil as his young bride Madeleine, and Marilu Henner as the unsinkable Molly Brown. Peter Gallagher and Catherine Zeta Jones played a pair of love-torn passengers, and Tim Curry appeared as a thieving steward, bent on relieving customers of their valuables. *Variety* magazine was less than impressed, calling it "star-studded but hackneyed ... nothing allays one's suspicion that those fearsome rolling dark sea scenes were shot in a bathtub."

But James Cameron's movie *Titanic,* a Hollywood blockbuster for Fox, has breathtaking special effects. Writer/director Cameron, who made the hugely successful *Terminator* films, was so enthralled by underwater shots of the wreck that in the fall of 1995, he made a dozen descents to the bottom of the Atlantic in a special submarine to take extensive footage of the sunken ship.

Once again called simply *"Titanic,"* the movie (which has reportedly cost $200 million) went into production in 1996. Curiously much of the filming took place in Mexico — not an area noted for its icebergs. At Baja in Mexico, Fox built a huge dry dock, a massive replica of the *Titanic* and gigantic tanks for the underwater scenes and close-ups. One of the tanks, measuring 600 square feet and with a capacity of 17 million gallons, was used for filming the partially submerged replica minus the stern section. Scenes have also been shot at Halifax, Nova Scotia, the port that received the corpses of those who died in the disaster and where the 150 unclaimed bodies were buried.

Some of the most difficult scenes, including the collision with the iceberg, the liner breaking in two and her journey to the bottom of the sea, have been created using computer-generated technology. These scenes are interspersed with Cameron's more traditional film-making. Co-producer Jon Landau says, "The trick is to keep switching around and not give people the chance to study what you're doing too closely and start figuring it out."

The movie is essentially a love story featuring a wealthy socialite passenger in first-class (played by the rising star Kate Winslet) who falls for an impoverished young man (Leonardo DiCaprio) during the voyage. The cast also includes Kathy Bates, Bill Paxton, Billy Zane, Frances Fisher and Gloria Stuart.

Rumors that the film was running considerably over budget echoed the experience on *Raise the Titanic!* And the oft-claimed curse of the *Titanic* manifested itself when some 80 crew members were struck down with a massive case of food poisoning during filming in Nova Scotia.

The film, the musical and the intention of raising the ship, have all put the *Titanic* back in the news again, nearly a century after she sank. There may now be precious few survivors left living to tell the tale, but there is no shortage of enthusiasts eager to keep the legend alive. As long as certain questions about the disaster remain unanswered — and with the passing of time, it seems they may be destined to do so forever — there will always be widespread curiosity about the precise circumstances surrounding the sinking of the world's largest liner, in her time the showpiece of early-twentieth-century ship-building. As the new *Titanic* film's executive producer Rae Sanchini observes: "The *Titanic* is a subject no one will ever tire of."

JAMES CAMERON
From the maker of the **Terminator** *movies comes the latest and most spectacular film treatment of the* **Titanic** *story – so far.*

KATE WINSLET
In James Cameron's **Titanic** *she stars as a first-class passenger who falls in love with an impoverished young man.*

GLOSSARY

Aft Towards the stern of a ship.

Amidships In the middle of a ship.

Berth A ship's place at a wharf. Also a sleeping-place on board ship.

Bilge The lower inside hull of a ship, up to the point where the sides become vertical. This point is known as the "turn of the bilge."

Bilge-keel A fin which prevents a ship rolling. Bilge-keels are fitted to the outside of the hull on each side of the keel at the turn of the bilge.

Bow Fore-end of a ship from where it begins to arch inwards.

Bridge Raised platform from where a ship is steered.

Bulkhead Upright partition dividing a ship's cabins or watertight compartments.

Collapsible Boat made with canvas sides, allowing it to be collapsed for easy storage.

Crow's nest Barrel fixed at the mast-head of a ship as shelter for lookouts.

Davit One of a pair of cranes used for suspending or lowering lifeboats (Welin was the common maker).

Deckhouse Room built on a ship's deck.

Displacement Amount of water displaced by a ship immersed in it.

Dry-dock Basin where water has been pumped out to allow for shipbuilding or repairs.

Flanks The sides of a ship.

Forecastle (fo'c'sle) A short raised deck at the bow.

Forward Towards the bow.

Helm To steer. The helm is also another name for the tiller or ship's wheel.

H.M.S. Initial letters of the words "His (or Her) Majesty's Ship" which prefix the names of ships of the Royal Navy.

Hull The frame of a ship.

Keel The lowest longitudinal timber or iron plating on which the framework of a ship is built.

Knot Unit of speed equivalent to one nautical mile per hour (one nautical mile = 6,080 feet).

Muster Assembling of a ship's crew for inspection.

Orlop The lowest deck of a ship with three or more decks.

Port The left-hand side of a ship, looking forward.

Reciprocating engine An engine which operates with alternate backward and forward motions.

R.M.S. Initial letters of the words "Royal Mail Steamer." These prefixed the names of both the *Olympic* and the *Titanic*.

Slipway Artificial slope down which a ship is launched.

Starboard The right-hand side of a ship, looking forward.

Steerage Part of a ship allocated to passengers traveling at the cheapest rate (in the case of *Titanic*, this was third-class).

Stern The rear part of a ship.

Stoker Crew member who tends a ship's furnace.

Tiller The lever fitted to the head of a ship's rudder for steering.

Transverse bulkheads Partitions arranged in a cross-wise direction within a ship.

Trimmer Crew member who distributes the cargo evenly on a ship.

Triple-screw Ship with three propellers.

INDEX

PICTURE CREDITS

The publishers would like to thank the following sources for their kind permission to reproduce the pictures in this book:

AKG, London 12, 88-9. **The Bridgeman Art Library, London**/*The Titanic Sinking on 15th April 1912*, Harley Crossley 1991, Private Collection 62, 74-5. **Christie's Images** 38t,b. **Corbis-Bettmann** 14, 48t, 58t/UPI 48b, 58b, 65, 78, 107, 115. **Courtesy of the Cork Examiner** 4-5, 13. **Mary Evans Picture Library** 8t, 17t, 18, 77, 92, 95, 98. **John Frost Newspapers** 7, 27, 39, 67, 70r,l, 71, 82, 83.

Ronald Grant Archive 108, 110, 112. **Hulton-Getty** 30, 49, 81, 86, 96, 101, 104, 105b. **ILN** 19, 33, 91. **Image Select**/Ann Ronan 69. **Trevor Lawrence** 60-1. **London Features International**/CPS 125t. **MSI** 6, 55, 105t. **National Geographic Image Collection**/Emory Kristof 106, 116, 117, 118, 120, 123, 124 **National Maritime Museum, London** 25 **Paul Louden-Brown/Courtesy of** Ocean Liner Society 15, 34, 37, 40, 44, 45, 47, 56, 99, 100, 102, 103. **Robert Opie** 32. **Popperfoto** 10, 11, 29, 41, 42, 43, 51b, 52, 59, 72. **Rex Features Ltd.** 16, 22/Dave Lewis

125b/Sipa, Sachs 84-5. **Frank Spooner Pictures**/ Gamma, Merkel-Liaison 122. **Topham Picturepoint** 8b, 9, 17b, 23, 33tr, 51t, 54, 73, 87, 119. **The Vintage Magazine Co.** 20, 35, © Cyberflix. **All rights reserved.** 121

Every effort has been made to acknowledge correctly and contact the source and/copyright holder of each picture, and Carlton Books Limited apologises for any unintentional errors or omissions which will be corrected in future editions of this book.